YOUNGER VOICES STRONGER CHOICES

YOUNGER VOICES, STRONGER CHOICES
Promise Project's Guide to Youth/Adult Partnerships

Copyright © 1997, Kansas City Consensus

ISBN: 0-9658035-0-3

Publisher's Cataloging-in-Publication
(Provided by Quality Books, Inc.)
Leifer, Loring.
    Younger voices, stronger choices: Promise Project's guide to
    forming youth/adult partnerships / Loring Leifer & Michael
    McLarney. – 1st ed.
        p. cm.
    Includes bibliographical references.

        1. Youth volunteers in community development. 2.
    Intergenerational relations. 3. Junior League of Kansas City,
    Missouri. 4. Kansas City Consensus. I. McLarney, Michael. II.
    Title. III. Title: Promise Project's guide to forming youth/adult
    partnerships

    HN49.C6L45 1997   307.14'0835
                           QBI97-40500

Printed in the United States of America.

Cover and book design by Prime Media, Inc.
Illustrations by Joe Stites. Photographs by Robert Cole

For further information, contact:

Promise Project
c/o Kansas City Consensus
301 E. Armour Boulevard, Suite 605
Kansas City, MO 64111
Telephone: (816) 753-3398
Fax: (816) 753-6019
www.kcconsensus.com

we dedicate this book to Valerie Snitz. Valerie's enthusiasm, good sense, and willingness to speak out helped the Promise Project get off to a great start.

Contents

contents

Introduction

Teens in Sumter, South Carolina, didn't have anywhere to hang out and have fun after school, so they waged an uphill battle to turn an old warehouse into a recreation center. The New Horizons Teen Center has now become a national model.

Members of the Youth Ending Hunger organization in the U.S. collected 65,000 letters from young people around the world that were sent to world leaders to protest global hunger.

A high school environmental club in Maryland launched a campaign that resulted in much press attention criticizing planned legislation that would undermine forest conservation.

Multiply these examples by the thousands and you begin to get an idea of the creative power of young people. When given the chance and the support, they have proven that they can be the architects of social change. Today, young people are tutoring in schools, operating counseling hotlines, rehabbing inner-city homes, setting up computer systems, organizing protests, and running substance-abuse treatment programs. Together with adults, they are working to revitalize communities.

Bringing young people and adults together to improve their communities is the mission of the Promise Project, a joint effort of the Junior League of Kansas City, Missouri, Inc., and Kansas City Consensus. The Junior League is an organization of women committed to promoting volunteerism and leadership of trained volunteers. Kansas City Consensus is a non-partisan, citizen-based organization that gives citizens a voice in the public policy decisions that affect their lives. It focuses on helping Greater Kansas City reach its vision of becoming the Child Opportunity Capital.

These organizations have joined with agencies, businesses, and organizations to build new partnerships and shift the community's view of youth by actively engaging young men and women in leading, directing, and solving problems faced by our communities today. Under the umbrella of the Promise Project, youths and adults perform community service projects together, provide partnership training, develop plans to increase youth/adult partnerships during an annual retreat, and sign a commitment to implement their ideas so that they come to life through action.

introduction

The Promise Project develops partnerships between young people and adults that give youth a voice in decision making. These partnerships can be either formal or informal. They can embrace any type of community work that affects young people and their families. In some cases, this means that young people are brought onto boards or committees with adults, or help develop products or programs. In other cases, partnerships may mean that young people take action and seek out adults to serve as allies. In general, partnerships mean that young people are in roles formerly reserved for adults, and that adults are doing things *with* young people rather than for them.

Partnerships shouldn't be viewed as just one more separate program to be administered or added to, but should become an integral part of a group's mission. Partnerships are simply a way to improve what you do now by tapping into a new source of energy and talent. Although this book is focused mainly on how community organizations can start partnerships, the principles apply in any arena. Partnerships could work in schools, government, or businesses as well.

These partnerships are interpreted in many ways by each organization. The partnerships might not require any changes to your organization, just a change in attitude. The Kaw Valley Chapter of Habitat for Humanity was highly skeptical when a group of high school students from Shawnee Mission, Kansas, volunteered to build a home for a low-income family. Chapter officials couldn't imagine how a group of teenagers could raise the required $45,000. They didn't change the rules or the organization; they just agreed to give the students the chance to prove them wrong. A team of three students, in partnership with the school's nurse, mobilized fellow students, parents, teachers, and the entire community. A young single mother now has a real home for her two sons, and Habitat for Humanity has a new attitude about what determined young people can accomplish.

how to use this book
The book is organized around the principle of time. It starts with the argument for why an organization should consider starting youth/adult partnerships and continues with the process for making it happen. It is not meant to be read in a linear fashion. You can step in at any time. The information is offered in self-contained pieces.

The book is a guide for any organization that is interested in creating these partnerships. It will answer basic questions about why you might want to involve youth in your organization, where you start, and how you make it work. Topics include the benefits of these partnerships, how to assess whether your organization is ready, where to turn for resources, finding the right candidates, breaking the barriers, what youths and adults expect from each other, resolving problems, negotiating authority, generating creative solutions, and stories of how other organizations benefitted from partnerships.

a partnership trial
This book was written in partnership by a youth and an adult. The idea of such partnerships is so new that there isn't a lot of information available on the subject, so we used the book as an experiment.

Michael McLarney is a high-school senior. Loring Leifer was a high-school senior, so long ago that she refuses to say when. Michael is interested in writing, architecture, and exploring the outdoors. Loring is interested in writing, architecture, and staying indoors. Neither one of us had ever worked in a partnership arrangement.

Now we are experts. We learned firsthand about working together. We worked through issues and challenges in a series of letters (sent via e-mail) to each other, which you will find throughout the book.

Perhaps this book could have been written more quickly with only one writer, but it would not have been the same book, nor would the experience of writing it have been so enjoyable—and educational. We have a young person to thank for suggesting the writing partnership. Valerie Snitz, a young Promise Project volunteer who has since left for college, thought that if this book was going to encourage others to open the door to youth participation, we had better practice what we preach.

Thank goodness for Valerie. The book is finished now, and some remarkable things have happened. We laughed a lot. We shared stories. We both learned more about ourselves and the way we relate to the world. We became friends. We still write to each other.

We consider this experiment a success. Turn the page and find out why.

chapter one

FROM: Loring Leifer
SUBJECT: My Writing Partner Takes Naps

Michael, before our first meeting, I wondered as a solitary writer used to being the master of all my sentences, how would I fare with a writing partner—especially one who was 18 years old? What is reasonable to expect? Will you get bored with the project? Will you wait for me to tell you what to do? Will you resent my experience? I worry that I will tarnish your enthusiasm and make you cynical with the lessons I have learned. Will I wind up as your parent instead of your partner?

What if we have completely different ideas about the project? I immediately imagine the worst case scenario. Then I call you at 4 PM and in a voice fuzzy with sleep you tell me that you were taking a nap. What have I gotten myself into, I wonder?

FROM: Michael McLarney
SUBJECT: My Writing Partner Is a Task Master

I was on an expedition in southeast Alaska and had stopped for provisions. My friends and I were hungry and tired after being rescued from our precarious position 85 miles from food. We stopped at a hotel perched on the side of a mountain just above the icy waters of Glacier Bay. We resembled wild animals placed in the lobby sniffing around for food and reveling at the running water and flushable toilets.

From the hotel, I called my parents, who told me about the Promise Project job. Making the phone call seemed to drag me all the way back to Kansas City and civilization. At that time, it was the last thing I wanted to experience, but I had to consider the prospect of landing such a great job. Writing was a dream I had since I was a little child, when I produced my first book, Corvy and His Car. I didn't care exactly what I'd be writing as long as I was working with words.

I created a false image of you from Alaska. I pictured a woman who was very serious and work oriented, a sort of ascetic task master who was ready to put me to work at a computer station. I feared that I would be set in a hot office building with piles of papers and other busy work.

My excitement really overrode my fears because after a brief panic in the phone call, I smiled and thought that I could do any amount of work. I relaxed myself and knew certainly that the work would be fun so I would therefore be able to work endless hours contributing my heart and soul to a book. I sat on that thought for a while. I loved the word book.

Ciao, Michael

why bother?

a young mother brought her 18-month-old son to a doctor. She was very worried that David had not started to crawl yet. As they talked, the doctor observed that the little boy had a ball. Every time David would push the ball away, the mother would retrieve it and return it to him. The doctor suggested that she wait a while before picking up the ball. The next time it rolled away, the boy looked at his mother, waited a few seconds, and, when nothing happened, promptly *crawled* over to the ball.

"It's a miracle," said the mother.

No. It was just that when she didn't try to fill every need for her son, the boy realized he had to develop the skill for himself.

In our culture, adults make almost all decisions for children and then expect them to start out in the world at 18 as model decision makers—without giving them any experience in decision making. In a culture of prolonged childhood, it is not surprising that an 18-year-old cannot make good choices if he or she has not been allowed choices at age 10. Society expects children to act like adults without adequate preparation.

This wasn't always the case. In the past, teenagers led crusades, advised kings, commanded armies, and ruled empires. In these cultures, childhood crime, depression, and suicide appeared as rarely as lunar eclipses. In our society, where children are kept in a protracted state of dependency, these problems are as perennial as grasses.

The types of tasks assigned to youths indicate that young people are not expected to contribute to the welfare of the family or the community. They are expected to *follow orders*, not take part in developing them. Magazine articles abound on topics like "What's Wrong with Youth Today?" "Surviving the Teen Years," "Coping with Adolescents." This suggests that youths are a problem that needs to be solved, that they need to be *controlled* and *reshaped* into adults. This attitude locks young people out of community life and can make for an abrupt transition to adulthood.

The secret message communicated to most young people is that society, that is the adult variety, doesn't need them and will run itself without them until they too become all-knowing adults. Yet the fact is that society is not running itself nicely ... and the rest of us need all the energy, brains, imagination, and talent that young people can bring to bear. How foolish of society to think it can solve its problems without the full participation of even very young children.

We believe it's time to recognize just how foolish this is.

2

young people count

There is no shortage of well-intentioned community-building programs—that don't work. The commitment is there, along with the funding, and the talent. What is missing from this picture? One reason that programs don't work is they don't involve a significant segment of the community—young people.

According to a 1991 report from the U.S. Department of Health and Human Services, Office of Substance Abuse and Prevention, "In identifying the most essential elements for developing solid community prevention systems, empowerment is necessary at every level of society, from individuals, to communities, to families. Target groups must be involved in and develop their own programs. If your target audience isn't significantly involved in program planning and development—plan for failure." Imagine Procter & Gamble introducing a new soap without ever consulting the people who use it.

Anthropologist Ruth Benedict criticizes our culture for excluding young people from responsibility only to blame them for irresponsibility. "Young people cannot develop a sense of their own value unless they have the opportunities to be of value to others." Look at the "Just Say No" campaign, which is typical of society's attitude toward youth. Adults order youths to "just say no" to drugs without giving them the tools to make healthy decisions for themselves.

The negative news media image of youth as criminals or slackers encourages writing off young people as a group. Young people are not likely to be considered as competent individuals who can be interested in resolving not only those issues relating to them directly but issues of concern to the broader community. As a result, young people in our society easily become an under-utilized resource.

We allow stereotyping of teenage behavior in our media and in general conversation that would be offensive to most were it in reference to race or religion. Adolescents are segregated from the rest of society, put on hold, and told to be responsible, but given no outlets for responsible action. Adolescents aren't depicted as citizens of a community, and are even excluded from opportunities to practice citizenship.

Opportunities to exercise personal freedom and social responsibility are determined by age rather than demonstrated competence, and numerous legal restrictions limit the social contributions of youth. Therefore, regardless of individual abilities, children are often perceived as the incompetent possessions of adults, who must manage them "for their own good."

> "every time we teach a child something, we keep him from inventing it himself."
>
> – Jean Piaget

tap into a wealth of imagination, ideas and energy

Letting young people rule the world won't cure society's ills, but letting them have a say in how ills are treated might be the start of a healthier society. An 11th grader has valuable insights that an adult executive director will not have.

Our culture is waking up to the idea that unless young people are brought to the table to talk about what they think will solve problems and to work toward solutions, community-building efforts are laboring under a significant and unnecessary handicap.

More young people are serving on boards and making their voices heard. Organizations like Youth on Board, Youth As Resources, and Community Partnerships with Youth are at the forefront of this movement. They, along with the Promise Project, are discovering new ways to make youth/adult partnerships more effective.

If you are serving a particular population, you will do it better if you build your programs with input from the people you are trying to serve. Encouraging partnerships means that both youths and adults are accountable for what goes on in their community. Just as neighborhoods with a high percentage of renters are more likely to get run down than those predominantly owner-occupied, when more young people feel that they own their community and are responsible for its upkeep, they will treat it with more care.

Young people are capable of greatness beyond most adult expectations. Take Bill Gates for example. The founder of Microsoft Corporation and one of the richest men in America, Gates was only 13 when the Mothers' Club at his private school used the proceeds from a rummage sale to buy a computer for his class. In *The Road Ahead,* Gates remembers, "I realized later part of the appeal was that here was an enormous, expensive, grown-up machine and we, the youths, could control it. We were too young to drive or to do any of the other fun-seeming adult activities, but we could give this big machine orders and it would always obey. It's feedback you don't get from many other things. That was the beginning of my fascination with software. And to this day it still thrills me to know that if I can get the program right it will always work perfectly, every time, just the way I told it to."

Only when adults view and respect young people as resources from the time of their birth are we likely to create systems that in fact promote the well-being of young people. It's time to say to ourselves: *No longer will I let myself see young people as victims, dependents, and problems, but as actors, providers, and solutions. No longer will I see my work as TO and FOR youth, but WITH youth.*

Young people possess untapped capabilities that they would be happy to share. Sometimes, all you have to do is ask. When the Kansas City, Missouri, School District couldn't afford to pay professionals to upgrade 70 miles of cabling in four computer magnet schools, it hired students from Central High School to do the job. After two weeks of training in how to work with sensitive computer cabling, 23 students worked full-time during the summer, hoisting cable above ceiling tiles and securing it with drills. Working side-by-side with teachers, they also set up more than 1,000 computers—with software.

"To actually get your hands dirty with a teacher that has been above you, that helps a lot," says cable meister Reynard Zwiefel.

And, guess what? The project came in on time and on budget.

making the case for youth participation Just as successful businesses
make decisions based on what their customers want, successful organizations need to do the same. Nike doesn't design tennis shoes without talking to the athletes who wear them. Organizations too need to be aligned with their target markets. Only teens can tell you what is going on in their lives, what are the pressures they face. "If the problem is gang violence, you go to the teenagers—even to the detention centers—and bring those youths to the table. Anything else is seeds for failure," says William Lofquist, a consultant on youth development issues.

"If we don't give young people real decision-making authority, we are going to lose them," warns Lofquist.

In many cases, young people will listen more closely to their peers than they will to their parents or other adult figures. Most young people have an adult filter, a listening device that turns itself off when an adult starts to lecture. If you have a message that you want to communicate to young people, you'll have much better luck getting through if the messenger is another young person.

Involving young people in decisions is a way of showing respect, of saying their opinions and ideas count. To accomplish this, both youths and adults will need adequate preparation and training. Just appointing young people to an all-adult board and giving them full rights and responsibilities won't work unless they have adequate education in governance and trusteeship. There has to be a commitment to creating a youth-friendly environment and giving all members the tools they need.

Often, both young people and adults have to learn to let go of stereotypes they each hold about the other, insists Jan Obergoenner, youth development specialist for the Mid-Continent Council of Girl Scouts.

Young people must give up the notion that adults are domineering task masters who want to keep all command, and, on the other end of the spectrum, adults must acknowledge that young people have something of value to contribute. A trust for each other is needed, according to Obergoenner.

What does it mean to involve youth in your organization?

FOR YOUNG PEOPLE, this means:

- Making a commitment to take on new roles and responsibilities.
- Learning to cooperate with different kinds of people.
- Believing that you can make a difference in your community, then working toward that goal.
- Recognizing how much power and influence you can have.

FOR ADULTS, this means:

- Being open to the energy and insights of young people.
- Learning to work *with* youth, not for them.
- Listening to youth rather than telling them.
- Letting go of your role as a parent or teacher to share power and responsibilities.

"to carry the spirit of the child into old age is the secret of genius."

– Aldous Huxley

benefits of youth/adult partnerships

Bringing younger people into leadership roles within their communities has a myriad of rewards—for the youths, the adults, and the organizations themselves. You don't have to wait years to experience the benefits. The payoff is often immediate. Some benefits can be expected, others may come as a complete surprise. Some organizations go into youth/adult partnerships because they think it will be good for the young people only to discover that the real beneficiary is the organization. Here are some of the benefits for the organization:

- **Giving youth a voice often results in better programming.** It also adds to the credibility of an organization, especially those that purport to serve youth. The Urban Summit, an event staged in Kansas City to keep inner-city youths out of gangs, was successful because it involved former gang members who understood the issues. It attracted young people and adults from around the country and spawned several new programs to give young people an alternative to street gangs.

- **Bringing younger people into decision-making roles within the organization can align it more closely with community needs.** A program dedicated to serving young alcoholics isn't likely to be meaningful if its board members have no idea of the experiences and needs of its target group.

- **Young people can make fund-raising easier.** Having youth/adult partnerships can give your organization access to new sources of funds. Many progressive grant providers are now making such partnerships a requirement for funding.

- **Partnerships make for good public relations.** The media are always looking for good stories and what better story is there than youths assuming positions of responsibility in their communities.

- **Young people who get involved in community-building efforts will be more likely to remain active as adults.** This seeds the organization for the future. If members of an organization feel a real ownership, they are more likely to stay involved longer and to serve with more conviction, both of which will strengthen the group.

- **Involving young people in community life can be a means of mobilizing the participation of their caretakers as well.** In some cases, young people have convinced their parents or caretakers to get involved in organizations.

- **By giving young people a stake in their communities, you bring an additional source of ideas to the table and make community-building a more democratic process.** Young people see from a different vantage point that gives a freshness to their solutions.

- **Young people help ensure a future generation of individuals who care about their communities and have the background and skills to make a difference.** Those who get involved early tend to stay involved as adults.

Some of the individual benefits for youths and adults are:

- **Young people benefit from caring relations with adults in their transition into adulthood.** Sadly, many young people grow up without this support. These partnerships can be especially meaningful to young people who don't have close relationships with their own parents or caregivers.

- **Working in partnerships helps people to fulfill the human need to belong.** Everyone needs to feel that they are valued and their efforts are meaningful.

- **Youths benefit from being part of a positive peer group, which is one of the strongest attractions of**

youth participation programs for young people. The influence of youths over each other is legendary. Having an adult yell at you is viewed as the price of doing business as a teenager. Having a peer yelling at you is a different story.

- **Youths benefit from having control over their own destiny.** They get an understanding of what it means to be an adult. They grow and mature with the responsibility. Instead of feeling like mere victims of forces beyond their control, they experience the satisfaction of making positive change. It is through the performance of tasks contributing to the welfare of others that people develop a sense of personal worth and competence and learn to be nurturing and responsible.

- **Youths acquire experience for future endeavors.** They learn how to communicate and work with adults, how to plan and execute projects and how to get a group working together.

- **Young people can be effective teachers and role models.** In many kinds of positive learning experiences, youths can be the most effective teachers and role models for other youths.

- **Each generation gets a chance to learn something about the other.** Many people discover that their partnerships improve their own family relationships. Youths get to relate to adults more as equals and thus develop a more sympathetic perspective of what it means to be adults. Conversely, adults see young people in a new, and often improved, light. This tends to change their own view about their own children.

- **Young people can try on various adult roles, and internalize the norms, values, and expectations of the community and of society.** Youths benefit from having contact with adults outside of their parents or teachers. Dr. Stephen Glenn captures this notion when he says that kids today don't necessarily need more moms and dads, but they do need more aunts and uncles.

- **Adults find themselves energized by partnerships with young people.** Adults learn new ways of doing things. Often adults get too focused on why something can't be done. A youth is sure to remind them why it *can* be done.

- **Youths can help strengthen adults' commitment to the organization's goals.** They lend an immediacy and sense of purpose to a group.

- **Young people can help adults see themselves in a different light.** They have a natural talent for mimicry and for seeing the humor and absurdity of situations. Just ask any adult who has ever been mimicked by a child. A mother yelling at her daughter sees the child contort her mouth in exactly the same way in response. "I realized that my exaggerated expressions were keeping her from even hearing what I was saying. The moment of laughter diffused the situation and helped make me a better communicator—for the moment at least."

- **Youths can inspire adults to think more creatively, to get out of ruts and break old patterns.** Working with young people can help you learn new ways to think. Young people have a way of sending a current of energy into the air—or at the least some waves of laughter.

"people can be divided into three groups: those who make things happen, those who watch things happen, and those who wonder what happened."

- Woody Allen

who should consider partnerships?

These benefits of youth/adult partnerships apply to any organization, business, agency, or institution that involves young people. The youth/adult partnership idea can be applied in schools, government, and businesses, as well as in the non-profit sector.

Sometimes, the partnerships start in non-profit organizations and move into other realms as the members of the organization take their positive experiences to other areas of their lives.

In the following pages, you will see how partnerships have been adapted to a variety of settings. You will also see that partnerships require sustained effort and shouldn't be undertaken lightly.

FROM: Michael McLarney
SUBJECT: Making Macaroni

Our first meeting was in mid August on a steamy hot afternoon. You totally contradicted my task-master image. When you rode up for my job interview on your bike, it tipped me off that you were a lot more like me than I thought. I knew you were healthy, environmentally conscious. I had imagined you driving a gas-guzzling Lincoln Town Car. You were very friendly.

I tried to keep this in mind after I'd gotten the job and we had our first working meeting. I panicked when I saw the stack of books, papers, and folders that you had collected for the project. My first thought was this is an equal partnership and I haven't done anything! You've gotten a two month jump start. My role seemed still a little hazy. I had so many questions, and we were already starting.

I was actually pretty nervous. I had worked with adults before, but now I felt a little uneasy. I had not worked in true partnerships carrying the same weight as an adult. A message was playing in my head, you are subordinate, you are subordinate, you are subordinate …

After we sat down and drew up a division of labor, I felt a little bit better. This helped me to know exactly what was expected from me. You need to know that I am very oriented to following other people's directions, and I follow them exactly, too. I'm the kind of person who follows the instructions to the letter for making macaroni. If it says boil in 4 quarts of water, I measure out 4 quarts. This unconscious neurosis is the result of years of training.

Maybe if I had more experience in a partnership, I would be more forward in giving my opinion or in departing from the recipe.

FROM: Loring Leifer
SUBJECT: Call the Red Cross

I noted your panic when you measured the stack of research papers and your discomfort as I stared at you trying to assess your competence. There is so little history for youth/adult partnerships, so the Promise Project is going to be watching us to see how we fare. But take heart, I feel as much like a lab rat as you probably do. And I remember that feeling of having an adult watching your every move. When I was about 13 years old, I signed up for a junior life-saving swimming course sponsored by the Red Cross. As it happened, I was the only one who signed up for the course. So I had two instructors. They didn't have anyone else in the class to watch, so they both watched me. Now the more time you spend analyzing someone's swimming form, the more things you can find to correct. With no one else to watch but me, they started to get more and more detailed in their observations. They pointed out that my arm was bent at a 130-degree angle instead of a 160-degree angle. If there had been several people in the class, they would have been happy if no one drowned. I started getting nervous every time I had to swim. I wished that one of them would go have a sandwich or get stuck in the locker room. But, it didn't happen. So I guess we just have to jump in the pool and start swimming. Yours, under observation, Loring

models for partnerships

there are many different ways to get young people and adults together to share ideas. Young people can be appointed to board positions, task forces, or committees. They can serve in volunteer positions, staff positions, as planners, as evaluators, or in focus groups.

Sometimes, organizations introduce the partnership idea by forming youth councils or youth committees, or just inviting young people to attend meetings. These can all be springboards to full youth participation.

Partnership arrangements are distinguished from mentorships. Partnerships are about sharing information and ideas, not about an older, wiser person bestowing wisdom on a younger one. Mentoring implies a *leader* and a *follower*. One of the challenges of sustaining young partners is to avoid becoming a mentor or a parent, but to sit back and let the young people share *their* wisdom and ideas.

Partnerships can grow out of the vision of one individual—be it youth or adult—or the sustained mission of a whole organization.

The common thread in successful partnerships is that they involve young people in decision making. Just having token youth members does more harm than good.

The roles that adults might play in the relationship include:

- **Role model.** By acting in a manner that shows concern for others, both young and old, adults can set the tone for the relationship by providing guidance and appropriate boundaries (e.g. emotional, physical, behavioral) in the least restrictive manner. Adults should then model these behaviors themselves.

- **Authority/Control figure.** Adults may be responsible for the organization, but should be careful where they exercise authority. Keep it limited.

- **Trainer.** Share skills and knowledge, and help youth improve abilities. Help youth negotiate systems (e.g. board structures, parliamentary procedures, social systems, and other protocols).

- **Guide/Advisor.** Provide input, information, wisdom gained from experience; don't intervene in decisions or direct the process. If you give young people enough support to do the right research, usually they will come up with good decisions.

- **Cheerleader.** Encourage young people, help keep their spirits up during hard times, but don't rescue them and don't DO for them unless asked.

- **Worker/Resource.** Do work for them at their request and under their direction; help them accomplish their plans.

The roles that young people might play include:

- **Active participants.** Youths can participate as equal partners in the governing process.

- **Researchers.** Young people are in the best position to understand the problems and pressures of other youth. They can do research and assess needs.

- **Promoters.** Youth can be a powerful voice in promoting the organization's goals among their peers outside the group and in the community at large.

- **Ambassadors/Advocates.** Young people will pay more attention to messages delivered by another youth, so they can be the most effective way to reach this population group. They can also serve as advocates for the thoughts and feelings of other young people.

- **Spirit raisers.** The intent of partnerships isn't to ask youths to pretend to be adults, but to add a young voice to the adult perspective. A youthful spirit can enliven a group.

"children have never been very good at listening to their elders, but they have never failed to imitate them."

- James Baldwin

The ultimate goal of youth/adult partnerships is to bring young people into the planning and decision making roles at all levels of an organization. Indeed, if youth participation is to be successful at all, it must be seen as a relationship between adults and young people that is integrated into the normal affairs of the organization, rather than as one more program to be developed and administered.

Here are some of the roles young people have assumed in partnership with adults:

- Grant makers
- Activists
- Consultants
- Service providers
- Political lobbyists
- Board members
- Advisors

youth as grant makers
The National Crime Prevention Council (NCPC) launched the Youth As Resources (YAR) program to offer grant money to young people for community projects. In each community, a local board of directors composed of young people and adults develops the program structure and funding base. It can be operated as an arm of an existing foundation or set up independently. The purpose is to get young people involved in their communities.

Young people must design a project, create a budget, write a proposal, and present it to the board. The project must be associated with a local non-profit organization, whether a church youth group, a nursing home, an environmental organization, or a school district. YAR programs have included conflict resolution, substance-abuse reduction or education, and homeless programs.

In Baltimore, YAR is being coordinated through the community foundation. In Indianapolis, it began through the sponsorship of United Way of Central Indiana.

A school district in Kansas City is using the program to award grants to young people for doing community service projects. Started with a grant from a state program in Missouri, the Hickman Mills School District operation is run by a community board of young people and adults who will review and award grants to youth proposals that address community issues.

The project will also hire a part-time youth manager. "The young people have to come up with the project and make a proposal. Any group can apply—a classroom, a church group, or three youths in the neighborhood who want to clean up a park," says Suzanne Siler, safe and drug-free school coordinator for the school district. "Youths will have to make decisions about what programs they want to support."

This is a crime prevention and a substance-abuse reduction strategy. "Criminal or destructive behavior and substance abuse indicate an alienation from the community, from parents, family, or friends. The best way to prevent these problems is to help young people to connect with the community, to make sure that they feel they can make a difference," says Siler. "When kids aren't attached to their communities, they feel like they don't have a part. They are just observers. We are trying to foster connection as part of our prevention strategy."

youth as service providers
"If you don't give youth a voice in shaping programs, the programs are going to fail," warns Sherry Wood, project coordinator for the Johnson County Task Force on Drug and Alcohol Abuse in Kansas. The group's Teen Advisory Council wrote a *Community Action Plan* to treat substance abuse that involved surveying more than 1,000 teens. The task force runs a Juvenile Peer Panel, which offers monthly peer-to-peer education for young people ordered by the courts, and a Diversion Review Board that gives first-time offenders a chance to erase offenses from their record if they comply with the board's instructions. The TAC also operates a Teen Speakers Bureau; Teen Connection Hotline; Prom Night Promise, an awareness activity that encourages teens to sign pledges not to drink and drive on prom night; Week-end Camp-Out Retreats; and a Young Entrepreneurs Program, where TAC members are creating their own storefront business operation.

"Teens bring energy, openness, and enthusiasm to a youth/adult partnership. They usually have a clearer understanding of the actual attitudes and experiences of their peers than adults have, and at times they are willing to raise challenging questions that adults are reluctant to ask," says Wood. "They have access to their peers, and, when they choose healthier lifestyles and get involved in building healthier communities, they show both teens and adults that teens are capable agents of change."

"Sherry Wood gets everything going, but then turns it over to us. We couldn't do it all ourselves. She does all the important footwork, like getting grants and arranging places for us to speak," explains 18-year-old TAC member Lauri Paul. "She's instrumental in the whole process. Without her we wouldn't be where we are today. Knowing that an adult cares about the teens made it seem more interesting. The adults in the group are more like friends. If you need someone to talk to, they are there."

youth as board members
Often, young people are more ready to serve on boards than adults are prepared to have them at the table. Young people need to know how to function within an adult-oriented board, and adults need to know what they can do to make their board youth-friendly.

Youth on Board in Boston, Massachusetts, helps agencies overcome many of the barriers they face in recruiting and involving young people on boards. They work with 30 boards in Boston and another 120 around the country. Youth on Board requires groups that want youth board members to join its one-year BoardBlazers program.

Through BoardBlazers, Youth on Board provides technical assistance in areas like board structure and dynamics, bylaws and policies, mentoring, and liability. "The board culture will need to shift a little bit," says director Karen Young. "Our training puts direct attention on what life is like for a young person. They need the meeting to be more loose, for there to be relationships, and for there to be food. The result is that everyone has more fun and everyone benefits."

Like people in other human rights movements through history, young people need allies. It makes sense, Young says, to build relationships with adult board members. "The youth governance movement is starting with adults who really care about young people, making room for them and letting others know we need to do this," Young says.

In 1994, Synergy appointed the first young person to its board of directors, a 16-year-old who was the president of the group's Youth Advisory Council. "We are committed to principles of community youth development. That means you view young people as resources for change," says Carol Kuhns. She is the former executive director of the organization in Parkville, Missouri, that provides residential and emergency shelter for youth and family counseling services. "We are more responsive to needs of young people if we have their input. We make sure everything we do is youth-friendly. We had our Youth Advisory Council go through our emergency shelter program as clients so they could talk to us from a first-hand experience. They made recommendations about simplifying forms, changing language, and helped us redesign our client evaluation."

> "coming together is a beginning. keeping together is progress. working together is success."
>
> – Unknown

Synergy uses its YAC to train and nurture youth leaders. "In the fall, our goal is to elect another youth board member from the YAC. One thing we have learned: it's really hard to be the only young person on the board of directors. We don't have all the problems solved on how to incorporate youth, but we are working on it. Our first approach was to have our first youth board member participate only as a representative of the YAC. We are changing this to make sure that youth members are involved in all committees on the board."

youth as consultants

Since 1991, Youth Opportunities Unlimited, an outreach program in Kansas City, Kansas, has been offering school and community-based mentoring services and resource referrals, with offices in partner schools. "We place para-professionals in the three primary environments of young people: school, family, and neighborhood. They develop relationships and work with families on problems. They interact with them at school and interact in the neighborhood and make home visits," explains David White, executive director. Two young people from the organization's Youth Advisory Council serve on the board.

The YAC advises other businesses and organizations. Members worked with the Nelson-Atkins Museum of Art on the Henry Tanner exhibit, helping them develop a youth outreach education component. YAC members worked with the marketing firm of Jewell Baker Zander and with Blue Cross/Blue Shield to hold focus groups for Medicaid recipients. The firm developed a commercial based on their feedback. "They are available to anyone in the community who wants a youth opinion," says White.

youth as activists

Among many urban youths, walking away from a fight is perceived as cowardice. To turn this upside down and accord social status to turning away from violence, a national campaign is under way to deliver the message that real strength means using your head, not weapons to resolve conflicts. The "Squash It" campaign encourages youths to use a hand-signal—patterned after the time-out gesture in sports—that shows they want to control a potentially violent situation.

The mind-over-metal "Squash It" program relies on a mass media campaign and local community efforts all developed and run by young people. Locally, a youth council has spent about 2,000 hours promoting "Squash It" since it was brought to Kansas City in October 1994 by the Partnership for Children as a prototype for the national campaign. The "Squash It" Youth Council gets advice from adult sponsors and help when they need it, but youths decide how to sell the concept.

Council members, led by 26-year-old Michael Ruiz, have spoken to dozens of area schools and community groups and helped to create a complete marketing campaign. They've written songs, taped public service announcements, started an information hot line, and created posters, billboards, tee-shirts, and a pre-movie slide show.

Most of the local "Squash It" youth council come from the gang experience themselves and have been either witness or party to extreme violence. "All the guys I looked up to are dead or in prison. I don't know if I'm going to get shot or killed. I may run across a rival gang that doesn't like what I am doing," says Ruiz, a former gang member turned peace negotiator.

Sixteen-year-old member Chris Hill says, "I choose to live positive. I think about consequences. I always ask other kids, *What about next year? What about ten years from now?*"

youth as lobbyists

A group of teenagers from Sandwich, MA, wanted to discourage other students from smoking. They got together with William Sangster, a health education teacher at their school. For two years, the group lobbied the state legislature to enact a smoke-free public school law. They wrote letters and speeches, conducted interviews with the media, met with legislators, and submitted draft legislation.

According to an account by one of the students in *No Kidding Around,* after the first bill they helped draft was defeated, the students submitted a new proposal that included teachers and met the objections of the committee chairman.

"They wanted to see if we really believed in what we were doing, and I think we did real well. I think what really got their attention was our persistence," said Jeff Curry, one of the students. "We wouldn't take no for an answer."

The students walked the capitol building talking with every legislator they found. Two kids wound up having lunch with the Speaker of the House, who jumped on the bandwagon.

"The kid power was incredible," says Sangster. "The outcome was unprecedented. The House of Representatives overruled its own committee chairman and passed the legislation. It was the only major piece of legislation ever passed in the history of the Massachusetts legislature by kids—sponsored directly by kids."

"I must say, that day every one of us grew up a little," said Lynn Terrill, another student.

Curry believes their efforts had a real impact. "Especially in our class, the number of people who smoke is far less. There aren't many smokers at all."

youth as advisors
Those not ready to leap into full youth participation might consider starting a youth council. Although youth councils are a way to give young people a voice in organizations, they aren't partnerships because they generally don't give young people any decision making authority.

A youth council acts as an advisory group to an organization, making recommendations on youth issues to the board of directors. These councils provide a vehicle to influence decisions and activities regarding young people. They can provide input for funding, research on community concerns, and advocacy for youth issues, as well as undertake service projects. Many churches have youth councils that coordinate activities for young members of the congregation.

Councils can be organized by any group or agency—or young people themselves—at any level of community activity. It might be sponsored by a county or city, neighborhood, organization, or school. The only requirements are a sponsoring group and funding.

Flexibility is one benefit of youth councils, and their structure can be as simple or as complex as the organization allows. Youth councils generally set their own agenda. This can include monitoring youth programs, offering training and leadership seminars to other young people, raising money, gathering information on the needs of young people through community surveys, offering youth activities, or advising other groups on youth policy.

Youth councils give young people the chance to interact without the pressure of adults in the room. It can be worthwhile to bring young people together for youth-only conversations, even if you don't form a structured youth council.

"most of us become parents long before we have stopped being children."

- Mignon McLaughlin

chapter three

FROM: Loring Leifer
SUBJECT: A Typing Lesson

We've only had one working session and already I've learned something. When you were sitting next to me at the computer, I realized that I automatically took control of the computer. Why should this be a given? So, I insisted that you sit at the keyboard. I noticed that you couldn't type as fast as I could and that you liked to talk about your ideas before recording them on the computer. This made me crazy, because I feared one of your good ideas would be lost, so I couldn't resist leaning over and typing in a few words. Pretty soon, I skootched my chair closer to the keyboard. Finally, you stood up and said gently, "I think it's O.K. that you type. You are a better typist, and you are already inching toward the keyboard anyway."

You weren't fooled by my artificial attempts to put you in the driver's seat. While I am twisted in the mechanics of interpersonal interactions, you did the sensible thing and stepped aside to my speedier fingers. I wonder what other wisdom you will share?

Yours, at the keyboard, Loring

FROM: Michael McLarney
SUBJECT: A Driving Lesson

I think it's hilarious the way you psychoanalyze our relationship. It's like seeing myself through your eyes. You wanted to put me in the power seat for a while, since everything we've been reading says that adults need to give young people more power.

The first time I drove a car, I was about 11 years old. My dad and I were at our farm in Smithville, Missouri. The Saab crept its way down the gravel road with me behind the wheel. I laughed but kept my solid concentration on holding the steering wheel straight. I held my head high to look over the dash-board. At four foot five, I could barely see over the dash. I sat on my dad's lap, and he controlled the pedals.

"All right! Would you look at that! You're doing it. You're driving a car," my dad praised. I smiled at the thought of me being in control. I thought I was too young to steer. I thought that a kid my age couldn't handle that kind of power. Boy did I show them. I could do it! Anyway, I appreciated your attempts to let me steer.

Yours, Michael

at the starting line

You don't learn to drive by riding in the passenger seat. If adults want youths to become responsible drivers, they need to give them a chance to steer. Both sides are going to have to make an effort to adjust to the other. For the adult this means stepping back and for the youth this means stepping up.

Three important conditions must be in place for successful partnership efforts:

• Adults need to be willing to share their power and responsibility.

• Young people need to be willing to take on responsibility.

• And both need the skills to work successfully together.

These three conditions aren't so easy to create. Adults are often reluctant to give up power. They are used to taking responsibility for young people and are conditioned to work *for* youths, not *with* them. To work with them means giving up some authority and control. From the other side, youths often mistrust the intentions of adults. If they suspect that an adult is trying to trap or trick them, they may refuse the partnership when it is offered. Also, youths who have been brought up not to volunteer their own opinions in the presence of adults might be uncomfortable with assuming this role.

For youth/adult partnerships to be successful, they should be based on realistic expectations. An organization that invites young people on board and expects business to go on as usual is destined for disappointment. So will one that includes young people without being prepared to listen to them.

These partnerships require extra attention and extra training, for both youths and adults. Young people should be able to express their full potential in supportive and safe environments. This may require preparation from both parties. Both may have to let go of some biases and modify their outlook.

There are four different types of organizational or internal support needed for effective youth participation. They are:

• **Logistical support.** This includes staff time, meeting space, office supplies, administrative support, and money.

• **Acknowledgment, encouragement, and advocacy.** Sponsoring organizations

18

can support youth participation projects by publicly acknowledging what the young people are doing. This lets the young people involved know that their work is valued; helps change the community's perceptions and expectations of young people; and shows the community that the organization is concerned about youth issues.

- **Training.** Both young people and adults need skills to develop new relationships. At first, they may be awkward with each other. Adequate training is essential to help both to move forward.

- **Follow through.** Unless the organization is prepared to see plans through to completion, young people can get the message that their ideas aren't really valued.

a checklist for partnership preparation Before embarking on any partnerships, your organization should be prepared on the following fronts:

- **Forget everything you have ever thought about young people as a group and start treating them the same way that you treat adults.** If you follow none of the other advice in this book, just try this one. See what happens. A young man who might have been regarded as a slacker became an ardent animal activist when one of his teachers, who belonged to an animal rights group, stopped to ask what he cared about. A surly eighth-grader who liked to play tricks on her fellow Girl Scouts became a responsible project leader when a crafts teacher recognized her artistic talents and involved her in planning projects for the troop. A group of "typical teenagers" became a highly effective organization when one of their fellow students was killed by a drunk driver and the principal encouraged them to turn their mourning into a sustained commitment to increase penalties for driving while drunk.

- **Make a long-term commitment.** Encouraging youth involvement is an ongoing process that will have long-term effects—both positive and negative—on the organization. Don't decide to try it just because you think it might be a nice idea. If the young people don't feel that their contribution is taken seriously, you will alienate them. And, unhappy customers tend to be vocal about their negative experiences. One youth can tell 100 others. That can make recruiting more young people difficult.

- **Involve youth early.** Don't design a program and then invite young participants to critique or implement it. Ask them their opinions before you start. Let them define their own contribution. Consider forming a youth council to set up guidelines to decide in what ways young people might be involved in your programs and activities.

- **Involve more than the "stars."** Reach out to a broad spectrum of young people. Don't rely on only the traditional youth leaders. Serving is a great leveler; you don't need to be an athlete or the smartest student. You only need a willingness to serve. There are willing youth in every neighborhood, with valuable perspectives to share.

- **Develop a clear vision.** Determine the level of support desired in the community and then work to increase it. Try making youth/adult partnerships a permanent part of the organization's mission statement.

"a group becomes a team when each member is sure enough of himself and his contribution to praise the skills of others."

- Norman Shidle

19

- **Get parents or caretakers involved.** If you are considering youth participation, have a plan for involving their parents as well. If nothing else, this will make it easier for the young person to participate. Having support for their activities can help increase young people's commitment and can also help with logistics of getting to meetings.

- **Put someone in charge.** Most organizations that are actively involved have at least a part-time coordinator working to recruit, train, and support young people.

- **Tokens are for subways.** Young people have to be more than a name. Youths can detect make-work projects and will be alert to being tokens. Don't sit a young person down to count out 500 kidney beans if you are selling them by the pound. When they figure it out, you will have lost their trust—and their patience. Place them on important committees and give them resources and assignments, so they can carry a full load.

- **One is not enough.** If at least two young people (preferably three or four) serve on a board or a council, they can work together to develop confidence and ideas and to identify common needs. Youths tend to get intimidated by adults. If they have another youth with whom to share anxieties, they may stick around longer. Even if you have a pool of extraordinarily confident and assertive young people in the organization, invite several youths to participate. The right balance of youths to adults will differ depending on the tone and intent of the organization, but just one is never enough.

- **A place of their own.** Like adults, youths appreciate having a sense of possession, a feeling that something belongs to them. They should have their own space, something which they can decorate and organize.

- **Cultivate the right attitude.** Unless you are really open to letting young people have a say in decision making, partnerships aren't going to be meaningful. More efforts fail because of bad adult attitudes than lack of aptitudes. Young people are highly sensitive to adult moods and perspectives. If they sense unwillingness or resistance on the part of adults, their own determination will diminish. Be willing to learn and grow and spend time on the relationship.

CASE STUDY: 4-H advisory committee

The 4-H clubs had always been for young people, but the level of input by young people varied from one group to the next. A 4-H organization in Kansas City had a long history of adult domination. In 1990, the 4-H Advisory Committee for Eastern Jackson County underwent a major shift from an all-adult board to a predominantly youth policy board (except for an adult treasurer). "During the process, some of the adults had trouble giving up the reins. A small percentage of very active families quit when young people began to make decisions," says Leon Moon, a 4-H youth specialist.

The shift turned out to be good for the organization as a whole, though. "4-H is my organization because young people run it. There used to be an adult president and vice-president. Now, youths run the 4-H Congress. We take responsibility," says Becky Bratney, chair of the advisory committee. "If adults are running it, it's not for us. Adults used to run the organization and we lost a lot of young people because of it."

testing the waters

If you are considering bringing young people into the decision-making process of your organization, consider holding a discussion group where you explore the group's attitudes toward youth participation. Topics of discussion might include:

- Barriers to youth participation. What might make it difficult for young people to participate, e.g. meetings during school, transportation needs.

- Benefits of youth participation in the program planning, operation, and evaluation.

- Dangers of not involving young people.

- Generational stereotypes.

Questionnaires are a good way to begin discussion on the idea of youth/adult partnerships. On pages 22 through 24 is a self-assessment to gauge leaders' individual attitudes about youth/adult partnerships.

Adapted from *The Technology of Development* by William Lofquist, a youth/adult partnership consultant and trainer, the inventory is designed to give adults a look at their own assumptions about involving young people in the organization. It identifies a spectrum of attitudes that exist in all human relationships. At one end, people view others as objects, in the middle as recipients, and at the other end as valuable contributors or resources. This can be a starting point for discussion.

inventory of adult attitudes and behavior toward young people

Instructions. Based on the opinion scale below, respondents should select the level that best describes his or her own belief or approach regarding each statement and place that number next to it. See next page for scoring instructions.

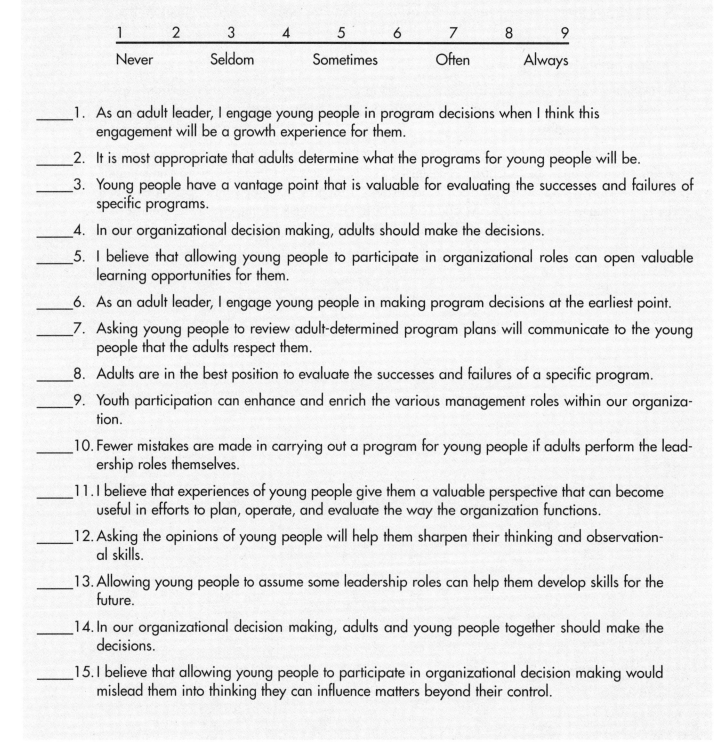

1	2	3	4	5	6	7	8	9
Never		Seldom		Sometimes		Often		Always

_____ 1. As an adult leader, I engage young people in program decisions when I think this engagement will be a growth experience for them.

_____ 2. It is most appropriate that adults determine what the programs for young people will be.

_____ 3. Young people have a vantage point that is valuable for evaluating the successes and failures of specific programs.

_____ 4. In our organizational decision making, adults should make the decisions.

_____ 5. I believe that allowing young people to participate in organizational roles can open valuable learning opportunities for them.

_____ 6. As an adult leader, I engage young people in making program decisions at the earliest point.

_____ 7. Asking young people to review adult-determined program plans will communicate to the young people that the adults respect them.

_____ 8. Adults are in the best position to evaluate the successes and failures of a specific program.

_____ 9. Youth participation can enhance and enrich the various management roles within our organization.

_____ 10. Fewer mistakes are made in carrying out a program for young people if adults perform the leadership roles themselves.

_____ 11. I believe that experiences of young people give them a valuable perspective that can become useful in efforts to plan, operate, and evaluate the way the organization functions.

_____ 12. Asking the opinions of young people will help them sharpen their thinking and observational skills.

_____ 13. Allowing young people to assume some leadership roles can help them develop skills for the future.

_____ 14. In our organizational decision making, adults and young people together should make the decisions.

_____ 15. I believe that allowing young people to participate in organizational decision making would mislead them into thinking they can influence matters beyond their control.

Inventory scoring instructions. Transfer the numbers given to each statement in the style that contains the box for that statement. For example, if you put a four by the first statement, then put a four in the box under the Style 2 column. In statement two, the number would go in Style 1.

Total the numbers at the bottom of each column. The one with the highest score is the one that best characterizes your attitude toward youth.

Statement	Style 1	Style 2	Style 3
1		☐	
2	☐		
3			☐
4	☐		
5		☐	
6			☐
7		☐	
8	☐		
9			☐
10	☐		
11			☐
12		☐	
13		☐	
14			☐
15	☐		
Total:			

Here's how Lofquist defines the three styles:

Style One: People Viewed as Objects. The basis of this attitude is that one person or group of people "knows what's best" for another person or group of people. The first person or group may decide they have a right to determine the circumstances under which the second person or group will exist. The person being viewed as an object usually knows it. In an extreme case, the adult sees little value in the young person except as the young person serves the desires of the adult. As a result, the adult controls the young person to serve whatever interests the adult may have. Less extreme is the attitude that adults know what is best for young people and see young people as the objects of their good intentions. This is not an uncommon parental attitude.

Style Two: People Viewed as Recipients. Here the first person or group still believes they know what is best for the other, but they *give* the other the opportunity to participate in decision making because it will be *good* for the other person or group. Thus, the other is supposed to receive the benefits of what the first person gives to them. An example of this attitude can be found in an organization that includes youth participation in the design of the program, but keeps the primary emphasis on how the young person will benefit from participation and not on what the young person has to offer to the group. This attitude demonstrates a concern for preparing young people for the *future* as responsible decision makers. This relationship cannot really be described as an adult/youth partnership, though there is some opportunity for the building of a sense of youth ownership in the outcome of decisions.

Style Three: People Viewed as Resources. This attitude is based upon respect for the contribution young people can make to the community in the *present*. It acknowledges that any leadership and decision making roles involved can be shared by adults and young people. Here there is an attitude of respect by the first person or group toward what the other person or group can do. This attitude and the behaviors which follow it can be closely associated with two matters of great concern: self-esteem and productivity. Creating a culture in which people are viewed, respected, and involved as resources is a worthy goal.

Young people should be regarded as resources not recipients, subjects not objects. "The purpose of youth participation is not just to do something that is *good for youths*. It is to avail ourselves of the usually untapped resources and abilities of young people in order to better prevent and solve community programs," says Lofquist.

liability issues

In addition to the attitudinal considerations, there are certain legal and liability issues to consider before inviting youth participation.

Rosemary Podrebarac, an attorney at McAnany Van Cleave & Phillips, explains that liability issues are governed by state law. Different states have different rules concerning when someone is considered a minor. "According to K.S.A. 38-101 in Kansas, you have to be at least 18 to be considered competent to enter into binding contracts. The period of minority extends to all persons under 18 or married persons at 16, regarding contracts, property rights, liabilities, and the capacity to sue and be sued."

For example, if your group wanted to start a substance-abuse program that required renting space and hiring a director, these constitute contracting acts. Thus, an action which was decided by a youth vote would not be legal. If you can't bind yourself, you probably can't bind the organization, according to Podrebarac.

"However, if your state statutes allow youth under 18 years to serve as directors, then their vote would be legal," continues Podrebarac.

Podrebarac adds that minors can assist in the development of mission statements and direction of policy. They could also serve as ex-officio directors or on advisory boards that would give input on projects and the direction of the organization.

> "teachers must be not only teachers but also discoverers."
>
> – Sten Nadolny

In some states, there are statutes that prevent someone under 18 years of age from being the deciding vote on a significant policy issue, such as firing an executive director. Thus, some attorneys advise that young people have full voting rights except for personnel issues. That was the approach taken by Youth Opportunities Unlimited, according to David White, executive director.

"Because the young board members were chosen from the Youth Advisory Council, the group didn't want young people to have access to the personal business of the YAC coordinator—her salary, benefits, or background. We felt this was an unnecessary exposure for the paid coordinator to have," explains White.

Limitations on the rights of young people are being challenged. Synergy gives its youth board member full voting rights, as do Kansas City Consensus, and the Girl Scouts.

"As adults who support youth liberation, it is important that we don't wait for the courts to grant young people rights. We need to encourage them to start acting as if they have them, and the courts will follow. Young people need to have the experience of being powerful in a positive way," says Jim Senter, chairperson of the grassroots National Child Rights Alliance, which crusades to change the status of youth from property to persons.

"History shows that the courts follow the changes that are made in the streets. Civil rights laws didn't come until after there were sit-ins, demonstrations and people willing to stand up for themselves."

If you are considering a youth appointment to your board, you should approve voting procedures to be used and decide what kind of memberships will be granted to youths. These might include:

Full members. Youth can join all discussions, serve on committees, participate in all board events, and vote on all issues. A slightly more cautious approach would be to record votes as either youth or adult. In the case of a tie, it would have to be broken by the vote of an adult. This keeps young people from having the deciding vote.

Committee Members. Youths can serve and vote on all committees. Then an adult board would ratify committee decisions so that youth participation would be supported by a legal vote of the board. Ask youths to represent the committee at the board meetings and make committee reports. While this doesn't not give young people official board status, it does give them influence in decision making at the committee level.

Ad-Hoc Members. Ask the youth to serve in an ex-officio or ad-hoc capacity. Youths would be able to join in discussions, serve on committees, participate in all board events, but they would not vote on issues. This will be the least desirable arrangement to young people, as they will resent being told their input is valued, but not enough to get the right to vote.

Before deciding, check with your local attorney or contact the Constitutional Rights Foundation for a copy of the booklet, *The Role of Youth in the Governance of Youth Service Programs.*

On the plus side, there are no age restrictions on directors and officers (D&O) liability insurance policies, says Tom Hogan, an independent agent who specializes in insuring not-for-profits. "It doesn't matter whether someone is 75 or 15 when it comes to writing a D&O policy. What that policy does is protect the board and the organization for liability issues, such as failure to perform. For example, if the executive director didn't buy public liability insurance and someone falls on the premises and there is no coverage, the board and the executive director could get sued. The D&O policy would cover them for suits regarding failure to act in a prudent manner. Most policies extend to officers, directors, volunteers, and employees," says Hogan.

"Where you get into age requirements is in automobile insurance," he continues. "It's extremely difficult to get automobile insurance for someone under 25 to transport people in behalf of an organization." Of course, individual youths can get automobile insurance, but it's not a good idea to put them to work as drivers, owing to the difficulty of getting insurance.

celebrate your commitment to partnerships Now that you are
ready to leap, make the event a celebration. Hold a ceremony, send out news releases, spread the word. Consider having each member of the organization sign a declaration of their commitment to the idea of youth/adult partnerships. Here's a sample declaration based on the one we use at the Promise Project. Feel free to adapt it to your own organization.

THE DECLARATION:
creating partnerships between youths & adults

I accept the invitation to generate partnerships between youths and adults that involve young people in decision making. I believe young people should have a voice in our community. I am committed to creating partnerships because I believe that young people are resources for today, rather than in some distant future. I believe that partnerships between young people and adults provide benefits for both, as each learns from the other. I assert that our families, schools, and communities will be happier and healthier when we are all working together.

I subscribe to these <u>guiding principles</u> for youth empowerment:

➡ Chances to Grow   I believe we must provide an array of opportunities for young people and adults to grow together as human beings by forming partnerships in the areas of decision making, leadership, advocacy, and community service.

➡ Valuing Diversity   All individuals are entitled to be treated with dignity and respect. I am committed to processes that reflect the equality of all people and that allow us to move beyond stereotypes to see what we have in common and what we can do together.

➡ Partnerships   I am committed to building partnerships among young people and adults, and I recognize that where adults are in power, they have a special responsibility to involve youth, and both need to be open to the experience of being equal partners.

To build partnerships, adults and youths have rights and responsibilities. I will work to assure that the youths and adults involved:

- Have access to the information, training, and experience we need to be full partners in decision making.

- Realize that each of us has a unique perspective and cannot speak for an entire group.

- Share ideas in ways that are true to our beliefs while communicating in ways that are understandable and respectful of others.

- Do what we say we will do as members of the partnership.

My signature shows that I believe in these principles, rights, and responsibilities and signifies my commitment to support youth/adult partnerships.

_____   _____
Name   *Date*

chapter four

FROM: Michael McLarney
SUBJECT: The Great Divide

Loring, my worst fear is that you would secretly hate my work and not tell me. If you would yell at me or start pushing me around, I'd know that I was doing something wrong. You need to be more critical of my writing. I learn more from criticism than acclaim. I can't be critical of your writing because you are a better writer than I am. You are a published author and have had more experience. You've learned more from your mistakes. We can't pretend that we are the same. Should we pretend that we are both famous authors? If we pretend that we are both on an equal level, we would be lying to ourselves. How can we change this situation?

I hope this letter will make you happy and appease your letter addiction. See ya soon! Hope you had a stellar weekend!

Soro soro shitsurei shimasu (that's Japanese for I apologize I'm going to commit the rudeness of leaving, but I hope we will spend leisurely time later), Michael

FROM: Loring Leifer
SUBJECT: You Be Shakespeare; I'll Be Dante

Michael, I think that the real spirit of this book should be the insights that we can both come up with about youths and adults working together. The intent of this project isn't for me to work with you as a teacher. You were hired for the position because we liked your writing style and the way you thought about the world around you, not because we thought you could be whipped into a William Shakespeare. I expect to learn from your observations about being a youth working in an adult world. The fact is I ENJOY reading your work.

I admit, if you made a criticism about my writing, I would probably appreciate it—as long as you didn't make too many. So I promise to make observations, if I think your work could be improved. But, this is the deal: you have to do the same with me. If you think I could improve upon my work, you have to let me know. Yours, in advice and occasional criticism, Loring

boot camp for partners

Youths want and need strong adults who can provide support and resources as needed without taking control from them. Adults are also essential in providing things young people cannot: reliable transportation, access to other adults in the community, and fiduciary authority. Most youths, to varying degrees, recognize that adults have something to offer in the way of experience as well.

And adults, also to varying degrees, recognize that young people have something of value to contribute.

Now the challenge is matching them in productive partnerships that will enable both groups to see beyond their own biases and stereotypes about the other.

Making the right match between youths and adults requires some careful choices. Give careful consideration to whom you put in charge of developing youth participation. Make sure it's somebody who has a rapport with young people and has trust in their abilities. Selecting the right adults who can provide support and encouragement is vital to the success of any program.

If you don't have a youth council or a youth group as a natural source for youth partners, then you will find yourself in the business of recruiting. In finding young people to participate, it's easy to look for straight-A students and student council presidents, but don't overlook the drop-outs and disenfranchised. By the sheer act of inviting them to participate, you may help them discover that they have something to contribute. In recruiting young people, you will be better served by having a mix of life experience, education, race, and gender, just as is the case with adults.

When adults need young people for an event or project, they sometimes call the Promise Project for help. Typically, their request is: "Can you send us some kids?" They forget young people have specific skills and interests, just as adults do, and that there are specific avenues for recruiting youths with the specific skills they need. They think they need a generic batch of youths.

Young people don't come in one-size-fits-all. You need to pick a young person based on the job to be done, much the way an employer would fill a position. If you want a fresh view, look for independent youths that aren't quite so traditional in their perspective. Look for colorful, animated, and even youthful characters. If adults look for carbon copies of themselves in youths, they won't benefit from a new perspective. A position that involves speaking to groups won't necessarily require a National Merit Scholar, but a gregarious youth who is comfortable with others. In hiring a youth to work on this book, we wanted someone who could stick with a project over a long period of time, who could express himself well, who spent time thinking about issues.

So now that you've got the right attitude and are committed to bringing more young people into your program, *where do you go to find them?*

When the women's movement was just beginning, women wanted to serve on boards and committees like their male counterparts. Often, though, men on the boards didn't know how to locate women who were interested in and ready for board service. So talent pools were created to give boards access to qualified women.

The Youth Talent Pool. The same resource is available today for organizations that want to include young people. The Promise Project and the local chapter of the National Conference of Christians and Jews together have developed a pool of young people with leadership experience in their schools. The members of the Talent Pool are offered additional training, and are matched with organizations based on their interests.

Ann Jerome, former executive director of the Camping Connection in Kansas City, called on the Youth Talent Pool when her organization wanted to diversify its board. "As the organization is involved with youth, raising funds to send underprivileged youths to camp, we thought that having young people on our board would be one way to accomplish this. The Talent Pool helped us locate youths that would be interested in an agency that works with camping activities. We got about 25 applicants from the pool. We narrowed it down to four young people, all of whom are on the board now. They started in March 1996. So far, it is working well. The young members have the same voting privileges as the adults."

thoughts from Loring

Working with an 18-year-old writing partner is nothing like I imagined. From our first working meeting, Michael wants to get to the heart of understanding youth/adult partnerships, while I am thinking about how to include more bulleted passages because the committee seems to like them. He wants to talk about the core of the book, and I want to please the people who have commissioned us to write it. This makes me feel prehistoric.

When compiling a division of labor list, we are able to distribute the tasks between us in an easy and natural manner. Then I become determined to format the list with a box grid. As I am deep into trying to figure out how to expand my desktop publishing skills, I hear Michael's soft voice, "I think it is fine just the way it is."

He is right, of course. He has already discovered that I am a closet computer nerd who will spend five minutes writing a sentence and then 20 playing with typefaces—and he is trying to save me from myself. My perception of what an 18 year-old understands expands, and I breathe a sigh of relief that we are so well matched—a formatter and a finisher.

Talk to teachers and school counselors. Adults who spend their work lives with young people are a great source of information. They can tell you who the most committed young people are. Similar to adults, the youths who participate in the most activities at school are usually the ones most likely to make room for just one more. And some activities can apply toward the school's service learning or internship requirements, which can be an appealing perk to teenagers.

Clubs and networks. Match your group's mission with youth organizations that have compatible interests. If it's to clean up neighborhoods, maybe a youth-oriented environmental club would be a good start. If your city has a resource and referral network, this can be an efficient place to start. Informal networking can pay off, too.

Call religious leaders. Churches and synagogues often have youth groups or councils. Many religious institutions have already placed young people in decision-making roles in the congregation. First Calvary Baptist Church appointed two young people to serve on the nine-member youth pastor search committee. "We had a real voice in the process," says committee member Andrew Turley, a 17-year-old student at Rockhurst High School. At Temple Beth Torah, the Youth Group president, currently Todd Blackman, serves on the board of directors. "He reports on the group's activities each month and has full voting authority on the board. One of the benefits is that the adults are more informed about youth life in the congregation," explains Mark H. Levin, rabbi.

Computer bulletin boards are a great place too. Lots of creative young people spend time on the computer. Post notes on local bulletin boards and computer forums frequented by young people. Invite them to attend meetings. Be as specific as possible as to your needs.

Consider the children of your friends. You are probably already well-versed in their aptitudes and accomplishments.

Don't pass over the young people whose leadership abilities may be hidden. Don't ignore the wild child. Sometimes, the smart-mouthed, irreverent rebel can be channeled creatively. Of course, getting this person to join an organization can be a challenge.

Young people are more likely to get involved if they are approached by another youth. One teen is more likely to trust another teen than an adult. Peer pressure is a more powerful motivator than parent pressure.

Interest is more important than skills. According to Albert Einstein, "Imagination is more important than knowledge." Skills can be learned, if the interest is there.

CASE STUDY: from one side of the law to the other

Lauri Paul's first experience with the Diversion Review Board was not when she was invited to serve, but when she was ordered to appear before it. The DRB gives first-offenders an opportunity to have their sentences erased if they comply with the DRB contract. After having been picked up for possession of marijuana, the 18-year-old Paul agreed to attend a meeting of the Teen Advisory Council, which sponsors the DRB. The board is composed of two adults and two teens. (The council, sponsored by the Johnson County Task Force on Drug and Alcohol Abuse, Inc., works with the spectrum of issues related to alcohol and drug use.)

"I didn't know what to think, but going to the meetings was better than going back to court," says Paul. "I came for my first meeting at Christmas time in 1994, and they were wrapping presents at Kmart to raise money. I wrapped presents there a couple days and have been involved ever since. I could see that the kids were making a difference. When I was really starting to get involved, my friends said it was stupid and pointless. We aren't friends anymore. I graduated from Shawnee Mission West High School, and I'm taking a year off to work before going to college. I work as a check-out supervisor at Kmart, and I've made a lot of new friends.

"Serving on the TAC has taught me a lot. When I'm talking to a manager, I can be on his level and know what he's thinking. But when I'm talking to someone my own age, I know where they are coming from. I also have the satisfaction of knowing that I'm helping other teens. It's helped me become more patient with people and able to understand where people are coming from. It helps me see both sides of a story—how the adult feels and how the kids feel too."

asking the right questions
Here are some questions that adults might ask potential youth partners:

- If you could do anything to make your community better—no limits—what would you do? What keeps you from being able to accomplish this?
- What would have to happen or change to make it possible for you to work with adults to improve the community?
- What kind of support would you need from adults?
- How would you define partnership?
- What are the challenges in working with adults?
- When you disagree, how do you resolve differences?
- How do you see your role in the future as an adult volunteer?
- What special skills do you have that might help the organization?
- What can you do that adults cannot do?
- How are you different from an adult?
- What kind of authority do you have over your own life?

Here are some questions that young people might ask adults:

- What can you tell me about your organization's goals?
- What will be expected of me in the way of time?
- How will my participation differ from that of the adults?
- What kind of training will I get?
- What happens if youths and adults are divided on an issue? How do you handle conflicts?
- What does the group expect to gain from these partnerships?
- In what ways do you plan to involve young people? What roles do you envision for us?
- What kind of problems can I expect?
- How do you define partnership?
- Will I get to vote at meetings?
- How will you assess candidates?
- What scares you about the arrangement?
- How will we evaluate the success of our partnership?

"there are two ways of spreading light. to be the candle, or the mirror that reflects it."

– Edith Wharton

train, train, train
Now that you've found your candidates, the next step is training.

chapter four

Although to the greatest extent possible, young people should be treated in the same way as adults, they will need an orientation to their assignment, because this will often be their first committee or governance experience. This would ideally be a personal meeting that allows the new members to get to know the staff and other volunteers. Young people, like adults, need to know what the organization is and does. What is the mission and what is expected of the members?

For some partnerships to work, young people have to learn what is like a foreign language—the language of the boardroom. They need to become familiar with boardsmanship, parliamentary procedure, and rules of order, which are likely to be completely new ideas for them. Board skills can and need to be taught. They must be oriented to the history and structure of the board or commission. They need to understand legal, liability, and budget issues. Consider allowing the young people a voice in determining the kind of training they will receive.

Make sure training is adequate and relevant to the needs of young people. As this may be their first foray into community service, they may need more time to acquire new skills, such as planning and decision making, conflict resolution, communication, goal setting, public speaking, community organizing, and public relations. Time spent training pays off in the long run. These skills will help them reach the organization's goals, just as any board development program would.

Don't forget the adults. These partnerships will be just as new for the adults. Adults may know Robert's Rules, but they may have no clue how to support young people. While young people need *skills* training, adults will need *relationship* training. They need to know what to expect from youth involvement. What can adults do to integrate young people into the organization? Even if the adults are adept in board procedures, they will need board development training to determine how a board that now includes young people will work together.

Community Partnerships with Youth, Inc. [CPY], is a pioneer in training young people for community and board service. CPY, based in Fort Wayne, Indiana, offers two training curricula, Youth as Trustees and Youth in Governance. The trusteeship curriculum inspires community service; the governance curriculum provides training on the administrative functions and day-to-day workings of a board of directors. Both are interactive and skills-based. (The Promise Project is among many groups around the country that CPY has trained to present their curricula.)

"If you're a member of a Boys & Girls Club, you see the rules come down," says Anne Hoover, CPY executive director. "Once you're on the board you see that you have responsibility for creating those rules."

Any first-time board member will need to learn the procedures and language of a board of directors. Hoover tells about the time that an adult and a young person were asked to research an issue prior to a board vote. The adult wasn't going to be able to make the board meeting, so he gave Devin, the young man, his proxy. "At the board meeting, Devin spoke up when it came time to vote and said he had the adult's proxy and would vote for him. It was empowering moment for Devin. He knew the language, what it meant, and he was charged with a responsibility—which he could do with ease because he had good preparation."

The Promise Project offers two programs to orient young people and adults to the idea of partnerships: the Partnership Retreat and "Partnerships 101" training. It also offers the Youth as Trustees and Youth in Governance curricula that was developed by the Community Partnerships with Youth.

The Partnership Retreat. During this two-day retreat, young people and adults work together as peers to begin to put youth/adult partnerships into place in their organizations. Eight groups are invited to each summit, and each group sends eight participants—five youths and three adults. Participants explore their shared past and examine current trends. They talk about the roles they have played in youth/adult partnerships. Participants create a picture of the future they hope to achieve and develop specific steps to make that picture a reality.

"The Partnership Retreat helped us think about how we want to include youths in the development of Science City," says Shirley Esher, education program coordinator at the Kansas City Museum. "We created a plan to develop a youth advisory group. We don't want static exhibits, we want interactive *environments.* We've held focus groups with young people, and we've gone to several high schools asking young people to brainstorm on creating such environments. If you were going to explore prehistoric Kansas City, what would you want to experience? During a session on exploring the human body, one young participant suggested following an aspirin on its course through the human body."

High-schooler Jared Shirck attended his first Partnership Retreat with the Science City group. Today, he serves on the governing boards of both Science City and the Promise Project. He says that young people involved in Science City have polled people about what they want from the museum and reviewed architectural and schematic plans. "We came up with the idea, which will be used, of having one part of the building be like the inside of a body," Shirck says. "That's a few million dollars right there."

Shirck agrees that the Partnership Retreat changed the role of youth in Science City. "The Partnership Retreat gave Science City a clear idea of the future of youth involvement. They realized they could create a structure of youths and adults working together and separately. Five years from now, when the entire museum is running, I think it'll be one of the biggest youth/adult programs in the country."

> "one of the things i've discovered in general about raising kids is that they really don't give a damn if you walked five miles to school."
>
> – Patty Duke

"Partnerships 101" training. The 101 training is a fun, interactive way for groups of young people and adults to explore how they work together. The two-hour training centers around the idea that we can view others in one of three ways: as objects, recipients, or resources. Once adults can identify how they view young people, and vice versa, change comes rapidly.

Just talk to Leslie Stelzer, PTA president at Prairie School and an educator by profession. When the PTA decided to bring sixth graders into decision making, Stelzer asked the Promise Project to provide the Partnerships 101 training. Fifty sixth graders and about a dozen adults got hands-on experience working in partnership. The reaction from the sixth graders and adults was optimistic. The sixth graders said they had learned "you can get along with adults," and that "adults probably feel the same as kids." Several said they realized they could be leaders. Adults said they "liked learning more about youths and being surprised by their insights," and that they "learned how important it is to listen to young people." At the end of the training, participants worked in small groups to role play how they want to treat one another.

Now students are making decisions about PTA programs and activities—to the delight of all involved.

Synergy, a non-profit group that operates a residential and emergency shelter for youth in

Missouri and is involved with the Promise Project, saw first hand the importance of training after appointing its first youth board member. "Any board member will need training and support. But you don't have to do so much with adults because they've often had other board experience," says Carol Kuhns, former executive director of Synergy. "Young people don't know parliamentary procedure or Robert's Rules of Order. You've got to spend time with the basics. The training of a young person shouldn't be different than the training of any person who has never served on a board."

ready, set, go You've got the right attitude, found the right partners, and provided the right training. Now you are ready for action. Here are suggestions for a smoother ride:

- **Getting to know each other is crucial.** Take extra time to let the young people get to know others in the organization. Adults can operate with certain assumptions or trust that don't necessarily exist between adults and youths. Youths may need more time to feel comfortable because they are the ones operating in a new theatre. A successful beginning depends on having idle time to talk over the project and get to know your partner. This means discussing the project at hand, but also talking about general things such as family, friends, and hobbies. In most

---

CASE STUDY: hey day for PTA

"We've all kind of been coded or socialized to think of adults carrying on certain roles and sixth graders carrying on other roles. I wanted to break some of those stereotypes. I wanted six graders to participate in PTA on a planning level, not just having events planned for them," says Leslie Stelzer. She approached 10 of the 30 PTA committees on the subject, and all ten agreed to welcome young members.

"Before we did this, I wanted to get some training," she says. "About 50 out of 80 kids signed up when the PTA asked for volunteers."

Prairie School will never be the same. Sixth graders now serve as the master of ceremonies and script writers for the school variety show (formerly adult jobs). Youths serving on the Art Smart Committee decided to keep the school decorated. Young people on the Outreach Committee helped decide who would make appearances at the school, then served as their hosts. And Prairie School sixth graders put together a proposal that raised $500 for Project Prairie, the centerpiece of the school's service learning curriculum.

Project Prairie is a natural habitat that includes a pond, gardens, and an historical schoolhouse. The sixth graders took responsibility for providing four compost bins. Class member Molly Cobb worked on a committee that identified Wild Oats, a local health food store, as a potential funder.

"We put together a presentation, we put together important points about why this would be good for them, and we practiced a lot," Cobb says. "We didn't ask them for any amount of money. We told them the total and asked if they would contribute something. We thought maybe they'd contribute $100, but they thought it was such a good idea, they gave us the whole $500. We were so surprised and happy, we had a celebration." Since then, the committee got the whole school involved in decorating the bins. The committee's bin sports the Wild Oats logo surrounded by butterflies.

"Given the opportunity, they thrive," insists Stelzer. "The sixth graders are 11 and 12 years old. This is just the time when peers start to take precedence over adults. If you can get them oriented toward positive risk-taking, you'll alleviate the possibility of negative risk-taking. This gives them opportunities to use their talents in a positive way."

"We could be doing this with even younger kids," challenges Stelzer.

partnerships, there will be a slew of working time, yet one of the most precious is the first meeting. There is a need to set aside an hour or more so that adults and youths can get to know each other. [See exercises in the chapter on "Recipes for Success" that can be used to help this happen.]

- **Buddy up.** Almost all organizations that rely on youth participation insist that youths fare better if they have one adult to whom they can turn for questions or concerns. A buddy system can integrate young people into the organization more quickly and provide them with a less-threatening information channel. Facing one adult is a lot less intimidating than facing an entire pack of them. Having an adult partner builds cohesion and allegiance and increases young people's comfort level.

- **Take a capacity inventory.** Record the special skills and interests of each young person and each adult involved in your organization—writing skills, sports abilities, knowledge of special subjects. This can be used when you allot resources to organizational activities or make decisions about future endeavors in the community. Make sure to share this information with the whole group.

- **If you want your meetings to be more productive, distribute written materials ahead of the meeting to all members with topics for discussion.** As young people are less likely to be familiar with subjects like budgeting and capital expenditures, they may need more research and background materials. A board buddy should walk the less experienced member through the first few packets. An experienced member can help the youth recognize significant information.

> "minds, nevertheless, are not conquered by arms, but by love and generosity."
>
> – Benedict de Spinoza

- **Avoid acronyms and technical jargon in written and oral communications.** Aim for using plain English. Avoid the buzz "ing" words of non-profits like "initiating, actualizing, advocating, prioritizing." These words don't mean much to young people (or to most adults outside the non-profit sector as well).

- **Define roles and assignments clearly.** The first crucial task is to establish each other's jobs. What is the scope of work? What decisions will be made? Who will make them? How much time is required? The stress of the unknown is usually worse than the reality. Before the long haul begins, partners must know what they are hauling and how much weight they are going to pull. Make sure that each task assigned is tied to the organization's goals. Members should know just what is expected of them and how the assignment fits into the big picture. Young people seem to fare better with more structure. Let's say an organization is trying to research liability issues surrounding a fundraiser. It might be enough to assign a task to an adult that is as simple as "Bob, find out what the liability issues are." As young people are used to specific instructions in school, the vagueness of this request makes it easy to ignore. You would have better luck getting the youth to take action by saying, "Before next week, call the law firm of Chasing, Suing, and Settlement and ask if there are any special rules for holding a fundraiser in a school building."

- **Assign activities as equitably as possible given the time constraints of members.** Make sure that the fun tasks and the drudge tasks get divided fairly between adults and young people. Don't just dole out menial tasks to youths, thinking that they will do better with the *easier* duties.

- **Let young people determine the pace.** In a study of successful youth-adult relationships, researchers found that adults in satisfying relations allowed the youth to drive the relationship in content and timing. They waited for the youth to show when trust was established and to divulge personal information, to define the adult's role. In unsatisfactory matches, the opposite was true. A degenerative process began and young people stopped showing up for meetings and withdrew from the relationships.

- **Beat the logistics.** Transportation and meeting schedules can make or break youth involvement. Take into account school days, work schedules, and transportation costs when planning meetings and events. Arrangements should be made when activities are taking place during school hours and young volunteers should be encouraged to talk about their involvement with classmates and teachers. This encourages a cross-pollination of ideas and can add to volunteer power.

- **Be sensitive to young people's financial situation.** While an adult might have no problem laying out money for an out-of-pocket expense to be reimbursed later, young people might not have the income to permit this. Make sure that they get reimbursed quickly—or better yet are given money to make agreed-upon purchases beforehand.

- **Don't let hunger diminish commitment.** Attendance is always better when food is involved. Concentrating on the task at hand isn't as easy when your stomach is growling. Make sure that you have kid-friendly food at your meetings. (Diet soda and rice cakes don't qualify.)

- **Make time for fun.** If you expect people to volunteer their time for your project, it should be fun. Take advantage of the natural humor of people involved in the group. Groups need to be able to play together as well as work together. This is especially true of young people in volunteer roles.

- **Provide opportunities to develop skills.** Get young people involved in leading discussions, writing press releases, laying out newsletters, marketing a product. This will improve the performance of your organization and give young people skills that can be applied to many endeavors in the adult world.

- **Address the question of privacy.** Young peo-

thoughts from Michael

Walking into my first Promise Project committee meeting, this was only my second day on the job. As the group discussed the book, I felt I had nothing to contribute. I didn't know how much the group expected me to know. I wasn't ready for the meeting. I kept trying to think of something to give to the meeting. It was intimidating.

Walking into a room full of adults, I am immediately intimidated. I fear being interrogated. I have this picture of walking into a boardroom full of adults all in suits and me in my street clothing. I feel like the exception, the special kid who is not really there to work with them, but for them. I feel like I have to prove my worth and that they don't. They have nothing to prove, but I would.

It is hard to work under these conditions. Your creative process isn't likely to be on full drive when you are under the pressure of proving something—that you can work with adults.

If someone had told me just what was expected of me, I would have felt better. If they had said, "We know that you haven't had time to get to know the project, but we just wanted to meet you," I would have felt less anxious. Also having another youth in the room would have made it easier. When you are the only youth, you don't have anyone to ask.

ple need to understand that there is no need to reveal personal information about themselves, although they should be encouraged to speak from their own experience. They also need to have a clear understanding about what information on the organization can or cannot be shared with outsiders.

- **Sit down, back off.** Remember that when adults are speaking, young people are not. Be patient, ask them questions, and help them feel safe to speak their minds. Actively encourage young people to contribute during discussions. Consider giving them a turn in facilitating a meeting or planning an event and provide the training that will allow them to be successful.

- **Give youths information, not conclusions.** As Oliver Wendell Holmes once suggested, "Many ideas grow better when transplanted into another mind than in the one where they sprang up." Let young people develop ideas on their own. You can help by supplying information, but let them run with it. Sherry Wood, project coordinator for the Johnson County Task Force on Drug and Alcohol Abuse, has learned this lesson. "When members of the group's Teen Advisory Council would get carried away with the youthful exuberance of wanting to do something big, I used to say *this isn't going to work.* I've learned to say instead, *O.K., let's see what you need to do to make it work.* When the teens wanted to host an all-night Winter Celebration on New Year's that would be open to unaffiliated teens, I could see all the things that would have to be done, arranging adult supervision, renting a place, publicizing the event, having a plan in case problems arose, settling the liability issues. Instead of saying that I didn't think this was a good idea, I just listed all the things they would have to consider. What they would do if someone brought alcohol in? Their first reaction was to kick them out. Then I asked them, *how can you be responsible and put someone out who had been drinking?* They realized that this wasn't something that they wanted to do. They recognized that it was too big for them to do, too risky," says Sherry Wood. "But they came to the conclusion on their own."

- **Reward questions.** Both youths and adults sometimes won't ask questions when they are confused because they are afraid of revealing their lack of understanding or they think that they are the only ones who don't understand. People need to feel that they won't be mocked or criticized for asking any question.

- **Reward accomplishments—of all members.** This doesn't just mean a pat on the back either. Make the recognition public. Consider special awards, certificates or extra credit points (if the school is involved in the project.) The work of organizations can seem so abstract and the goals so far-distant as to become meaningless. Rewards help make successes more immediate and can increase motivation of members. It can also provide an opportunity for the support of sponsoring organizations to become visible to the community, and can help to strengthen the community's expectations for youth behavior.

- **Document your progress and provide ample time for reflection and feedback. Ask yourself: Are we accomplishing what we set out to do?** What should we be doing differently? What have we learned from our experience? How

"there are no misunderstandings; there are only failures to communicate."

– Senegalese proverb

do the members feel about their own personal involvement? If at all possible, build in ways to measure your success. Before you start a project, have a plan in place to track its progress. This means deciding what questions to ask of the people involved, at what intervals you will collect information, and what criteria you will use to measure success. Having documentation of success helps motivate participants of all ages, and, in times of reduced funding, being able to prove your success can increase your chances for survival.

Young people involved in healthy partnerships view themselves as leaders and potential leaders. They believe that their ideas and actions can change the community. They come from a variety of backgrounds and perspectives, and understand that they will not always agree and conflicts won't disappear. Partnerships are opportunities to face the struggles and conflicts, to stick it out, and make long-range commitment to building a healthier community.

FROM: Michael McLarney
SUBJECT: Abducted into a Cult of Adults

Loring, my Japanese teacher gave a talk to the class today on how it is easy to put verbal homework on the "back burner." My English writing teacher gave the class a lecture on how easy it is to put journal writing off until the last moment. My chemistry teacher emphasizes how easy it is to do well if you only study an hour every night. Every teacher tells me not to say manana, but today is too packed and tomorrow is too full. I have pots boiling over; I have burning Japanese; and I have college applications that are still in the freezer. And, where did I put that Promise Project? Ahh, I think I found it next to the bologna in the fridge. If I'm going to be a representative of youth, I'd better start pulling my weight. This is about the busiest time of my life, and I'm feeling stressed out.

One of the goals of our partnership is to raise the youth to a higher level of maturity, but I often worry that I am being too adultified by all these pressures. By learning from you, I may have become more mature. Is this a contradiction of our efforts, since the adult is supposed to be creating a partnership with a youth? If I turn out for our next meeting in a pinstripe suit, how will that affect our partnership? I know it is inevitable that the young will grow old, but, for the sake of the partnership, I'll try to keep in touch with my inner youth. I'll take up jive, sand paper my jeans, quit wearing collared shirts, and maybe quit shaving every day. Honestly, though, we shouldn't worry too much about these appearances because that's all they are. The only real thing that has happened is that we've become closer and that could be mistaken for mimicking each other's identity.

Your "mature" partner, Michael

FROM: Loring Leifer
SUBJECT: Your Mother or Your Partner?

You're so wise sometimes. I think you've touched on one of the perpetual barriers to partnerships. How can we keep our healthy differences, but each be positively influenced by the other? When I hear you complain about trying to juggle all the assignments in your life right now, I feel guilty, as if I am adding to your "adultification." Sometimes, I want to protect you, to keep you young as long as possible.

Other times, I try to prepare you for the adult stresses ahead and teach you the shortcuts—like using the same themes in papers for both your Japanese and English classes or asking your teachers to count your Promise Project writing as classwork, something you stubbornly resist as somehow cheating. I swing between wanting to disillusion you with my experience and trying to protect your youthful naiveté.

Several years ago, there was a French movie called "My New Partner" with Philippe Noiret as an old cop who knew all the angles. His days were spent working the system. When his old partner was sent to jail, he was assigned a new young, starry-eyed cop who still believed in living by the book—with no shortcuts. I feel like the seen-it-all old cop when I try to tell you how things work, when instead I should try to absorb your enthusiasm as an antidote to my adult cynicism.

Yours, hardened, Loring

we shall overcome —
the barriers

While the ideal situation might be a completely equal partnership where each contributed exactly 50 percent, in reality, it's near impossible. Have you ever heard of any kind of partnership—like marriage, for example—where tasks and responsibilities are split right down the middle?

Achieving absolute equality isn't the ultimate aim of partnerships, after all. It's to give young people real influence over issues that they regard as valuable. Aim for a healthy balance of differences. The goal should be tapping into each other's resources, not each trying to perform the same functions. You bring the enthusiasm; I'll bring the paper plates.

Young people can be full partners and should be treated as such. They should have decision making authority with voting rights. This doesn't mean that they have to perform the same functions or roles as adults. Adults, by virtue of their greater maturity and experience, may have more to contribute. The focus should not be on equality, but on the value of what each has to contribute.

Young people commonly will put more pressure on themselves to perform in partnership endeavors. As they are the ones being let into the group, they will feel more observed, more like they must prove themselves. They may need more assurance of their abilities.

partnership hurdles
Lack of parity is one of the pitfalls that you should be prepared to encounter in youth/adult partnerships. As the partnership idea is relatively new, the challenges are just coming to light. The good news is that solutions present themselves as the hurdles are identified. Here are some of the hurdles you might expect to encounter:

- **Transportation may be the number one barrier.** Even if adults are willing to drive, young people feel like a burden. Young people are dependent on their parents to get to meetings, but, as they near the prospect of getting their own drivers' licenses, they can also resent being dependent on their parents to drive them. Some organizations get around this by having young people organize carpools or "driving trees," where young people can call other youths who already have their licenses. Designated youth drivers might introduce themselves to parents and let them know about meeting dates. Be careful about the liability issues concerning young drivers, though, and remember you are probably legally safer not having formal transportation programs.

42

- **School is another challenge.** As most young people are unavailable during the daytime, they can't be involved in activities during this period. Often, they have numerous after-school commitments. While a working adult can make a few phone calls during office hours, young people generally do not have this option.

- **Incorporating youth into the process can take several years.** It can mean that programming suffers with the time spent on the learning curve. For the first few years, depending on the magnitude of changes, the organization may worry about reduced performance. Just as it is often quicker to "do the job yourself," involving young people can slow down some activities.

- **Young members are fleeting.** They have a funny way of turning into adults—very quickly. This may be good for society in general, but it can play havoc with organizations. You must constantly deal with training a new crop of members. Consider a *shadowing* process where young people recruit another young person before leaving the organization. A high-school senior could bring a sophomore or junior into the group and show him or her the ropes before graduating. Be careful, though, that this doesn't lead to cliques.

thoughts from Michael

It is hard for a youth to adapt to working with adults. We like to think that it is both the youth and adult who are trying to adopt to the other one's working style, but it is the adults who set the rules. Therefore, the youths have to learn new skills to follow these rules. Adults may disagree, but I think that youths have a greater challenge here.

- **Turf battles or cliques arise.** While cliques may be great for the people who are in them, those who aren't feel slighted. Also, people who join an organization together will also depart together. This can lead to wholesale migration if one member gets disenchanted. During meetings, make sure that everyone gets an opportunity to participate and that people are paired with a variety of others for specific projects.

- **Young people tend to take adults very seriously.** Most youths don't expect playfulness from adults. An off-the-cuff remark to another adult isn't so serious, where one made to a youth who isn't expecting it might be hurtful. Youths hold adults more accountable than we realize, viewing them as all-powerful and competent.

- **Young people will look to adults for assignments, deadlines, and structure.** Young people naturally expect adults to set the rules, to give them tasks to perform. They aren't used to having any say in developing the rules. This can easily lead to a situation where adults assign duties and become de facto *bosses* or *parents*, which can cause young people to lose a sense of ownership over their work. The more young people are involved in setting assignments and structure, the more you will create a true partnership.

- **Young members can mean changing an organization's culture.** It can mean giving up drinking and smoking at meetings or events. The time and place of meetings may have to change.

- **Caught in the parent trap.** Most adults have conflicting desires to shelter young people and also to initiate them into the ways of the world. They feel an obligation to relate to youths as if they were their parents. They feel responsible for the young people and compelled to protect them from mistakes and to teach them about life. This sometimes precludes adults from listening to young people.

- **Adults tend to jump in too quickly.** Understandably, adults will feel a greater responsibility for the success of the partnership and will want to resolve any discord as quickly as possible. Several youths talking at once or arguing over an issue might make adults uncomfortable, but, if they can desist for a few moments longer, they might find that young people could resolve problems themselves and gain more confidence.

- **Both youths and adults sometimes each shut each other out.** When youths think that an adult couldn't possibly understand, they lose the incentive to try to communicate. When adults feel threatened they can withdraw into the familiar role of responsible protector instead of partner. These reactions are natural and expected, but everyone should be conscious of them because they can put up barriers.

thoughts from Loring

Periodically Michael talks about trying to prove himself to me, as if that were his and not my burden as well. "Why is it you adults are so competent all the time?" he asks. No matter how hard I tried to dispossess him of the notion or how much evidence I offer to the contrary, he continues to carry this burden alone. And I continue to tease him about it.

- **Both youths and adults tend to underestimate each other.** Adults should try not to rely on preconceived ideas about what a young person can (or cannot) do. It's better to let them show you. Conversely, youths shouldn't limit adults by assuming that they are narrow minded and controlling. Letting go of stereotypes will allow both youths and adults to be delightfully surprised, and both will enjoy the freedom to act as individuals without the burden of having to disprove stereotypes.

- **Youths and adults tend to regard each other as being from a different species instead of only a different generation.** Adults sometimes get so preoccupied with the pressures of behaving like an adult that they suffer amnesia about what it's like to be a teenager. And youths tend to think that adults can't possibly understand their problems, when, more likely, the older generation faced similar problems themselves.

- **Leadership gets confused with authority.** Working with young people as partners doesn't mean abdicating authority. It means learning to lead rather than to order. According to Ron Heifetz, director of the Leadership Education Project at Harvard University's John F. Kennedy School of Government, "Leadership is not a set of personal characteristics or an individual's role; it is the ability to meet an adaptive challenge, the gap between values and reality. It focuses work on resolving internal conflicts and contradictions. Leadership is about getting people to tackle hard problems and to not engage in work avoidance."

point/counterpoint
Because of these barriers, you may experience some resistance to the partnership idea. Here are some actual adult objections to youth involvement and suggestions for responding to them.

- **POINT: "Having kids at the meetings will screw up the open and honest discussions."**

COUNTERPOINT: At first, we may be uncomfortable about having young people present, but they may help us examine some of our perspectives and even become more aware of our biases. We might benefit from people who see from a different vantage point—and eventually feel more confident about our organization's programming. Keep in mind, too, that adults tend to behave more responsibly when young people are around. As a result, our board discussions may be more positive and productive.

- **POINT: "We need leaders in the community on our board, not kids."**

COUNTERPOINT: The most essential purpose of any organization is to accomplish its mission. While having community leaders on board is one method, having programs that are responsive to the people served is equally important. By involving young people, we can be more effective in reaching our audience, which can make it easier to attract community leaders to our cause.

- **POINT: "Young people are too irresponsible to contribute anything of value."**

COUNTERPOINT: People tend to raise or lower their performance to expectations. Young people don't have enough opportunities to be responsible. Let's give them the opportunity to surprise us.

- **POINT: "Having young people will slow everything down."**

COUNTERPOINT: There is a lot of preparation to paint a house the right way—scraping off old paint, spackling holes, sanding surfaces. You can just put the paint on without doing any preparation, but, in the end, it won't last as long as if you take the time up front.

- **POINT: "We won't be able to smoke or drink during meetings"**

COUNTERPOINT: Let's find out how many people would miss this aspect of our meetings. If the majority would miss this, maybe we can compromise. What about a smoking section in our meetings or confining a cocktail hour to 20 minutes?

thoughts from Michael

It is an almost irresistible impulse to let an adult take charge. If every youth was a General Patton, adults would surely pay attention to them. Unfortunately, a lot of youths are passive, which can often be confused with laziness or idleness. That's why we need to include youths at a younger age so that they develop an assertive voice with adults. As we will learn, the youth's voice is as important, if not more important, than an adult's.

- **POINT: "We'll spend all this time and trouble training young people and, after a couple of years, we will lose them to college."**

COUNTERPOINT: You have a point. Young people tend to become adults rather quickly. Some will return in the future to the organization as community leaders. Some will not. But keep in mind that adults don't serve on a board forever, either. If a young person is appointed as a sophomore or junior, their two or three years of service wouldn't be unusual for an adult board member. We can also look for ways that our young people become mentors for those who will follow them.

communication, the curse and the cure Ideally, communication is the
way to get over many of the hurdles listed above and to work through the objections to

youth/adult partnerships. Of course, it is also one of the biggest hurdles and needs to be given special attention.

Honest communication between adults and youths is often hindered because they feel uncomfortable in each other's presence. Young people are slow to trust adults. There are fewer givens. Youths are used to relating to adults as authority figures like parents, teachers, and bosses. In all these cases, youths succeed by respecting authority figures and meeting their expectations. They aren't conditioned to having expectations about adults. They have little experience talking to adults as partners. Conversely, adults are used to dealing with young people as their charges, not as their partners. Youths and adults may lack a common language.

When there is no common ground between the two, each finds it hard to connect with the other. Finding this ground may take time and may mean moving away from the business at hand. Youths must first recover from their negative perceptions of the adult authority figures in their lives.

When both youths and adults feel safe enough to talk about their problems with each other, then most of the other hurdles won't be as difficult to jump. And, each group won't be so concerned with testing the other.

thoughts from Loring

An infinite number of challenges can arise. Usually they are the ones that you didn't prepare for. Sometimes, they are just the opposite from what you predicted. Before we started working together, I worried if Michael would test his authority. Would he say the manuscript should turn right just because I said left? Instead, he waited for me to assign him a task with an earnest demeanor that suggested he would carry it out—no matter how preposterous it was. I discovered that my challenge was just the opposite. I would have to work just to get him to disagree with me. For the first several weeks, he invariably parroted my question, "What do you think?" with his own, "Well, what do you think?" My suggestions would inch toward the ridiculous. Ever gallant, he would pause for a few moments then respond, "Well, if that's what you think ..." I couldn't decide whether he was just humoring me or was afraid to test his authority by disagreeing. I had the feeling that in the comfort of his own family, he was much more animated, so I persisted.

who's the boss?

A ship captain is conducting his ship on the high seas late at night. It is pitch black and the seas are rough. The shipmate comes up and says, "Captain, captain, there are lights on the horizon."

So being no slouch, the captain immediately sends a message with blinking lights, "Change your course south immediately twenty degrees."

Not a moment goes by and there is some blinking light in return. "Change your course north twenty degrees."

Well, the captain is a bit perturbed by this so he grabs the signal, "This is Captain Smith speaking. Change course south 20 degrees at once."

Instantly, the message comes back, "This is Seaman First Class Jones. Change your course north immediately."

Well, the captain regards this as insubordination and in a fit of rage sends a final message not to be quarreled with, "Change your course south at once. I am a battleship."

The return message, "Change your course north at once. I am a lighthouse."

In partnerships there will be contests of will and power struggles. Testing one's authority is part of human nature. The success of the partnership will be determined by how each one responds to these contests.

Young people may naturally test their new authority.

Disagreements happen in all-adult groups. The difference is that adults may not take them as seriously. When one board member proposes 3 weeks of training and another says, "I don't think that's reasonable," the situation would hardly be noted. If a young person heard "I don't think that's reasonable," they might interpret the message as "Your opinion doesn't count."

Adults need to remind young people that it is perfectly acceptable to disagree with an adult colleague in a civil manner—then demonstrate the process. Adults need to be sensitive to the natural authority of their age.

While adults sometimes worry about power struggles, often it is the opposite that besets them. Young people are so oriented toward living under the authority of adults that they will wait patiently for orders. They are not naturally comfortable enough to disagree with the adults. Now many parents are probably thinking right now, "Hah, you wouldn't have that problem with my child." But the fact is that even children who swing from the chandeliers at home can become docile in the presence of other adults.

thoughts from Michael

The other day I was talking with one of my good friends about youth and adult relationships. She filled out a survey for me and gave it to me. Reading through this survey and all the others there was one common feeling among youths. All of them seemed to project that there is an intimidation factor. An eleventh grader, Christine "Bean" Schmidt, said that she is usually nervous when talking with adults so communication is a major problem for her.

Another, and equally serious hurdle, is that adults get carried away with the partnership principle and accept all youth recommendations, without applying the same critical process they would to an adult colleague's idea. Adults who give in too easily can set young people up for unnecessary failure, because an important control has been removed—examining and assessing ideas.

As with any different population groups, misperceptions are to be expected. Young people may regard the adults as out of touch or inflexible. Adults may view young people as immature and unrealistic. These perceptions need to be addressed—and tested.

FROM: Loring Leifer
SUBJECT: Victory at Last

After sharing one computer for several months, I didn't think it would be so significant when we found a place with two computers that permitted us to work side-by-side. The new challenge was that only one of us could work on the master file at a time. As the chief, but sensitive, typist, I promised that I would add your changes to the master copy. I thought this would be enough. I was so innocent when I left the computer lab to make a phone call. When I came back 15 minutes later to find you moved over to my computer—and the master file—my first reaction was "Oh my God, I've lost control."

Then I saw the work you had done. You wrote an introduction to a chapter that desperately needed one. Then I recognized a victory, "Hallelujah, he's jumped into the driver's seat." And we are both better for the ride. I wonder, do you relish the victory as well?

FROM: Michael McLarney
SUBJECT: And the Victory was Mine

Sitting and reading, I found numerous places that had errors that needed correcting and other places that needed writing, but I couldn't touch it because you had the master copy. I looked longingly at your screen.

"Michael, I need to make a phone call. I'll be right back," you said.

On your screen, the master copy shone with an incandescent light. I gave a furtive glance under my brow. "Good, now is my chance," I thought to myself. I stood up, fixed my collar, and sat down in front of the master copy. My fingers twitched eagerly above the keyboard before I started typing. I dove in and started adding to a section. Enveloped in my writing, I ignored your return. When you discovered me, I thought I saw you smile—or were you baring your teeth? I imagined that you might want to push me to the floor, but I wouldn't surrender my place. An equal partnership requires sharing, so hey, why don't I just stay here. I had tested the equality of our partnership, and you were still smiling.

recipes for success

Arecipe for success would be the most valued piece in a partnership. If we knew the formula like an equation, there would be no need for overtime. The answers would lie right in front of your face. All you'd have to do is plug in the humans. Unfortunately that isn't the case. Partnerships thrive on trial and error. People are all different and bringing diverse population groups together demands patience and determination.

In this chapter, you'll find tips and suggestions from others on how they made youth/adult partnerships work. We've included our own successes as well. Perhaps they can help ease the fit into a partnership relationship.

Success in a partnership is when both have the same vision. For example, we have a mutual vision that some day we will finish this book.

a packing list for success
Organizations already involved in youth partnerships say there are certain things you've just got to have. Here they are:

- Funds.
- A well-connected and open-minded board with lots of community network connections.
- Key funders who make youth decision making a criterion.
- A program that meets real needs and treats causes not symptoms. Search for the causes of problems and make sure solutions attack the causes, not just the problems. For example, substance abuse is often the symptom of underlying problems rather than the cause. One reason to involve young people in the first place is to identify the real needs of their peers.
  - A diverse mix of people, both youths and adults.
  - Youths placed in responsible planning and decision-making roles. Several organizations with working partnerships claim that it doesn't matter whether a young person wins or loses a vote, just that they must have say in decision making.
  - A defined process for choosing projects.
  - Host agencies for specific projects.

50

- A home base. This is especially important for young people to have a tangible place to congregate. Adults may have more experience with the idea of *telecommuting* than young people.

- At least a small staff.

- Ample training and technical assistance. Youth and new adult members will need special orientation to assume their responsibilities at first and continued training to deal with dynamic situations. Members should have somewhere to turn for assistance with questions or concerns.

- A process for documenting the success of projects.

- Good media relations. Make sure that the local media know about your partnership effort. Some people are more likely to patronize programs because they know that they are youth/adult partnerships. Let the world know through news releases and phone calls, regular mailings to other organizations and schools. Other ways to promote the organization include designing tee-shirts, posters, billboards, and flyers.

- Recognition of achievements.

creating an idea factory
And don't forget the most important—the right attitude. If you've got that, it doesn't matter that the chairs don't match or some of your board of directors wear Metallica tee-shirts and others wear suits. Attitudes—both on the part of

---

CASE STUDY: Mid-Continent Council of Girl Scouts

The Girl Scouts of the United States of America Constitution includes the admonition: "The troop belongs to the girls. Let them own it." The Girl Scout program is carried out in small groups with adult leadership and provides a wide range of activities developed around the interests and needs of girls. The organization encourages self-determination with a five-step program that gives members an increasing role in determining the plans and activities of their own troop.

"We held a focus group a few years ago, and the scouts said they liked making decisions. Those who quit or didn't join acted because they felt they didn't or wouldn't get to make decisions," says Jan Obergoenner, adult development specialist.

"It really makes you want to step out and take on more responsibility. You feel a sense of accomplishment," says Jessica Schnepp, senior Girl Scout. "Some kids feel intimidated to assume responsibility when the request comes from an adult. If a youth leader asks for young people to help out, they only need to ask once or twice."

The Girl Scout program believes that the benefits of a partnership are equally as important to the youth as they are for the organization. The youth gains the ability to perform tasks in society that teach her discipline and social skills, and lead to better self-esteem. It is proven that a child who is not taught how to interact in society at a young age is more likely to have problems later.

The Girl Scout program is successful because they work very ardently at overcoming many barriers before they are confronted. The most important factor, according to Obergoenner, is to break down communication barriers. This is a key element because for maximum working efficiency, the partners must feel comfortable sharing ideas and thoughts; they will not produce creative ideas in a tense atmosphere.

thoughts from Loring

Working side by side, I see that Michael is like the character in "Dr. Strangelove," who can't keep his hand from pressing the bomb button. Only with Michael, it's the delete button. He types a sentence, then runs over it with the delete button. He types two more words, then erases them. I glance over and see an entire paragraph. Two minutes later, his screen is blank. He erases more than he writes. He talks about an essay or a letter he is writing for the Promise Project—then he doesn't send it or can't find it. "Oh, maybe I erased it," he says. He knows that I fear losing ideas, while he carelessly drops them about—sure that, like a bus, another will be along shortly. At my age, ideas run fewer and farther between. I fear losing an idea—even a mediocre one.

Even if I smile at him while he types, he looks up and tries to second guess my expression. "I should take this part out shouldn't I?" he asks. Michael criticizes his work, flagellates himself for its inadequacy. He waits for me to criticize or judge his talent, while he accepts mine without question. He feels that he is working as a representative of all youth, that if he does poorly all youth will suffer. I work only for myself and recognize how much more pressure he is under to perform.

Slowly, though, he comes to understand how important his own contribution is, that I am happy to look beyond a few misspelled words or mis-started sentences to the ideas he contributes. I start to tease him about his delete-happy typing. And he teases me.

Now, when he says, "Oh, didn't I send that letter to you?" he looks sideways at me with a smile. We are starting to know each other.

adults and youth—are the main boost to youth empowerment.

One organization that leads the pack in youth empowerment is the Girl Scouts, a youth-dominated organization. The Girl Scouts place the highest importance on respect between youths and adults. Each project begins with the development of a mission statement, which must state exactly what the goals and plans are for the project or organization. The mission may even go further to state the division of labor. When the mission has been successfully established by both the youths and adults, both must concur on every detail from beginning to end, according to Jan Obergoenner, the adult development specialist for the Mid-Continent Council of Girl Scouts. She is in charge of training adults to work with youths and has become a specialist in the area of youth/adult relationships.

Obergoenner insists that there should be no difference between an adult relationship and a youth and adult relationship.

When you are dealing with two populations who don't have much experience in working together, attitudes and misperceptions can be changed dramatically. Erica Henry, a junior at Pembroke Hill, tells the following story. "At a movie, I changed places with an elderly couple so they could have better seats. After the movie was over, the wife came up to me and started crying. She said she had always viewed kids as insolent and irresponsible. She didn't know kids could be so considerate."

You want to establish a creative environment where each person feels like they are making a valuable contribution, where each feels comfortable and appreciated.

icebreakers
Here is a selection of icebreakers, games, and techniques for getting youths and adults working more creatively together. One problem in groups is that the few talkative people can overwhelm the rest. To help the shy come forward, play games where each person participates in turn. This helps everyone get equal time. These games sound silly, but that is exactly the point. Remember that being silly is a great leveler and a greatly undervalued creativity booster. It helps all of us transcend our own self-consciousness and youths to see adults in a more human light.

Round-Robin Idea Generation. One method for encouraging young people to participate in group settings is to have a method that allows each person a turn. A facilitator presents a problem and then gives each person present a few minutes to describe what he or she thinks would be a solution. Let's say the problem is teen suicide. You might get solutions like starting a hot line, providing counselors in schools, or talking to parents. After a list is compiled, then the facilitator goes back and asks each person what is the most essential purpose of preventing teen suicides? Is it just keeping teens alive or helping teens make an easier transition to adulthood? Or sparing parents this agony? These should be listed alongside the problem. Next the facilitator asks the group to look at how the solutions relate to the problem. Which solutions address the most basic problem of preventing the death of a teen? Which address broader issues of raising more well-adjusted adults? From here, the group can begin to decide what level the group might be able to reach and which solutions would best help reach this level. The round-robin method involves all participants in problem solving, even the shy person who might not speak up otherwise.

Partnership Poetry. Each person in the room contributes one line to a poem about what they hope to get out of the arrangement, but they can't start the sentence with "I."

People to People. In this energizing exercise, a facilitator instructs participants to find partners. Then the facilitator calls out combinations of body parts like "elbow to elbow," or "hand to back." When the person calls out "people to people," everyone has to change partners.

Getting to Know You. An effective mixer, this activity encourages youths and adults to get acquainted via word puzzles formed from the letters in their first name. Participants each write their name vertically on their own large piece of paper. Then next to each letter, they must list an attribute describing themselves that begins with each letter of their name. Like this:

L	=	Loyal		M	=	Mellow
O	=	Original		I	=	Industrious
R	=	Ribald		C	=	Comical
I	=	Incomprehensible		H	=	Hesitant
N	=	Not neat		A	=	Altruistic
G	=	Gregarious		E	=	Elderly
				L	=	Level-headed

After doing this, participants can pair off and discuss why they chose particular attributes. The cards can be collected and distributed at future meetings. Each person picks up their own card and then sits down with another member with whom they have yet to compare cards. Slowly, all the members of the group get to know each other.

Matching Meanings. Each person gets a card that either has a word or a definition taken from a board manual or an organization's charter. Participants then circulate to try to find the person who has a matching word or definition. When the group is paired up, they can be divided into teams and handed a board manual with the task of finding each word in the manual. Suggested words are: agenda, audit, by-laws, trusteeship, parliamentary procedure, budget, and strategic plan. In this way young people learn the language of non-profits.

The Lie-ability Game. Each person tells the worst lie that they every heard from an older person or a youth. Then they discuss why the person might have told it.

> "i know of no other way of dealing with great tasks than that of play."
>
> – Friedrich Nietszche

thoughts from Loring

I agreed to speak to a group of Paseo High School students as part of the Writers in the Schools program—at 8:30 in the morning. I don't think the students wanted to be there. My assigned topic was "Humor in Writing." You can imagine. They just stared open-mouthed at me. They didn't heckle; they didn't interrupt; they just stared. I was unnerved. We lacked a single common experience or denominator to share. I feared that they didn't like me. Later during a workshop, I asked them to describe the last argument they had and to exaggerate as much as possible. I gave them a list of insults taken from Shakespeare's plays to substitute for the four-letter epithets they might have used. When I showed an interest in their lives—and the difficulties or arguments they had with others—the students woke up. By involving them, I was able to tap into their thoughts and experiences.

The Argument Game. Same as above only participants are asked to describe their worst argument with a young person or an adult. This can be a great way to find out what kind of intergenerational conflicts need to be addressed.

The Talking Stick. In Native American cultures, the person who held the talking stick had the right to speak at a meeting. He had the power of the word and could speak his mind without fear of being interrupted or insulted. When he finished what he had to say, he would give the stick to whoever wished to speak next. Using a talking stick, a feather, a shell or some other object of significance is a great way to order discussions.

Five Minute New Idea Rule. New ideas are fragile. To encourage your membership to express them, consider a rule that no criticisms can be made of a new idea for at least five minutes after it has been proposed.

The Rule Finder. One person is designated as "The Finder." This person isn't told the rules of the game. (Be sure to pick someone who won't be rattled by having others laughing and not understanding the joke.) While this person is taken out of earshot, the rest of the group gets into a circle and is instructed to respond to all questions as if they were answering for the person on his or her left. If they don't know that person, they must guess how the person would respond. The Finder is then brought back into the room and told that the objective is to discover the rules of the game. Tell the finder that he or she can ask questions about anything other than the actual rules of the game and that each person will respond with the truth as best they know it. Although this game can lead to some tense moments, it can be quite revealing as to how others think of you. It can also expose biases that both youths and adults have about each other.

While games and exercises are effective icebreakers, real success depends on the culture that evolves over time. Fun should be built in to all of your organization's activities. When people are laughing and playing, they are more likely to be inspired and creative and motivated. If you don't happen to have the funds to pay everyone a salary in your organization, fun can be the next best incentive—for both young people and adults.

chapter seven

FROM: Michael McLarney
SUBJECT: Shakespeare Still Skateboards

My Uncle Mike told me about how he met his wife, Judy. They both worked in the same office building. My aunt was new to the job and vulnerable to the teasing and pranks of veteran workers—like my uncle. He placed a hose above her desk in the ceiling. Every day, he would let out a drip from the hose, which would drip onto the papers and files on her desk. After a few days, she pushed the huge wooden desk across the room to the other wall and placed a bucket on the floor to catch the water where her desk used to be. Pleased with herself, she went ahead with her work, but soon the ceiling started to drip over her desk again. My uncle had strategically moved the hose to another place above her desk. She moved the desk again, yet the drip followed the desk around the room. After a week and a half, my uncle broke into laughter when she commented on the mysterious drip.

After hearing this story, I laughed and thought to myself. You know what? This adult thing isn't so bad. Growing up, I have always seen adults as hard-working serious people. They didn't play games with each other, and they definitely did not mess around. I was wrong. As people grow up, they always have the wild teenager lurking inside them. Youths and adults really are compatible. It's just a presumption that adults and youths are very different. Adults may want the youths of the world to think they are all work and no play, but we all either know or will find out that everyone is still a kid at heart. Even you, Loring.

for young people only

growing up, you're taught to look up to adults and respect them. Adults become like idols. They teach you and show you the ropes of living in our world. Now you're a teenager and you may not want to be mentored by an adult. You may think you're finished being raised by adults and you want to break away. Your feelings are probably justified, but the answer is not to separate yourself and create a fissure between you and an adult. The answer is to move to another level of relationship.

Youths want to have separate identities from their parents, so when their parents try to imitate them, the kids get annoyed. When a kid tries to fit a mold at school and wants to be in style, that's O.K. When his mom tries to adapt to that style, it's threatening. Sometimes the styles are really stupid, like wearing your clothes backwards or leaving a tag on your hat, so when you see your parents doing this, you recognize how stupid the styles are. We should remember how fleeting fashion is.

Like they say, when you make your mark in the world, watch out for guys with erasers.

In an article, "Having Their Say," in *People* magazine (9/25/95), Carly Hammond, 14, expressed a very common sentiment: "I'm not the kind of person who's like, *I just want to make a difference.* A lot of people are like that. I don't want to be an adult. They're so cut and dried. I think once you get to be an adult, your brain shrinks. You stop knowing how to have fun. I never want to get married. It seems too routine for me. I hate routines, and I hate people telling me what to do, and I hate deadlines and things like that, so I probably wouldn't be too good at any job. But probably I'll get the hang of it."

My response is, Carly, adults won't bite. The greatest thing about being a youth is being a youth. You don't need to give that up to work with an adult. Becoming an adult doesn't mean turning eighteen. It's a choice you make sometime in your life. If you want to be a rambunctious free youth, then be it. Don't be too depressed when I say that deadlines, routines, and jobs are inevitable unless you decide to be a hunter and gatherer. Even then, though, you have a deadline to collect a certain amount of berries before you get too hungry. I strongly encourage that youths retain their free-spirited attitudes throughout their lives. Don't give in and become too serious. You can do well in school and gain respect of adults and still goof around. Trust me, if you make the grades, adults will give you more leeway.

As you age your brain will shrink. Your brain won't always be as alert as it is now. This is why adults would like to work with you. You serve as the drop of water that can rehydrate their overworked, dehydrated brains. Adults like youths for their free spirits. They don't want you to become too serious and dry. If you become too serious you lose your individual spunk and light that makes you shine. They want you to work with them as you are. If they wanted an adult there are plenty of adults to work with. Divert your energy and spirit towards your work, remain true to yourself, and you will be a success.

Remember, adults' brains may shrink, but they do gain some advantages with time. Here's a hypothetical situation. You're at the airport getting ready to fly to LaGuardia in New York and there are two planes with two pilots. You have the option of flying with the 47-year-old veteran pilot who flew in the Navy for ten years and has been flying commercial jets for another fourteen years. The other pilot is a fourteen year old kid that just received his license as a pilot because his wealthy parents own a small jet that he learned to fly. Pick your pilot and reflect why you picked the one you did. A recent poll showed that more people would pick the 47-year-old. The exceptions were a few people that either had death wishes or were members of a Parachute Society.

thoughts from Michael

"Take what you are offered" or "Don't cut off your nose to spite your face." It is interesting to analyze this aspect of myself because I tend to be bull-headed. I do not always take advice or services when offered. Through experience, I have learned one simple lesson that will help you out throughout your partnership and make things run much more efficiently: Take, take, take! When someone offers advice, criticism, or ideas, take them and accept them. Don't let your ego go to your head. We all need help. I learned this after spending three days trying to get a modem working before letting Loring help. So, take advice and use it. A partnership means that both parties will have to give and take advice.

tips and tricks for managing adults
Your relationships with adults will run more smoothly if you just keep in mind:

Criticism doesn't necessarily equate to condescension. Sometimes when adults offer criticism of a youth, they are just treating the youth the same way they would a colleague. Try to remember that adults are used to critiquing each other's ideas. Just because they don't agree with you, doesn't mean that they are dismissing you.

Adults may not be aware of how capable you are. Maybe they don't know any youths your age, so they just don't know what to expect. Or maybe they see you in the same light as their own teenagers who refuse to take out the trash. You can enlighten them by showing them that you are capable of handling mature situations. You can tell them a hundred times that you are mature, but showing them is the best way to make your case.

Adults will feel responsible for the success or failure of the project. This is what makes it hard for them to share authority over it. They need your reassurance that you are willing to share in both the successes and the failures too.

Adults are just as uncertain as young people, they have just learned to disguise it more. "I have positive interactions with youth on a regular basis," insisted one survey respondent. "Or maybe I delude myself."

pet peeves of adults
Here are the top complaints that adults make about youths.

You might want to keep these in mind if you are trying to get along with them:

- When youths are angry or disturbed and won't tell you that they are upset.

- Young people aren't realistic. They have big ideas, but don't understand all the work involved in putting them into action.

- When youths stall, put off doing work, or generally act lazy.

- When young people promise to do things that they can't possibly do or promise to do something and then don't carry through.

- Young people getting easily distracted and changing course, not being able to commit to one course of action.

- Youths refusing to hear or listen to adult experiences.

- Interrupting or being disruptive in a group by snide comments.

rewards for your efforts

The benefits of working in a partnership with an adult are not always under your nose, but if you have patience, the benefits are sure to appear. Working in a partnership with an adult can give you a much better understanding of what you will be experiencing very soon. They may start out seeming so different from you, but you will probably be amazed at the similarities. It can give you more respect for adults as well, which will help you in relationships with other adults—like your parents, teachers, and bosses.

This eases the transition to adulthood for young adults. You'll find it easier to talk to adults. You won't be so intimidated when you apply for jobs in the adult world.

Partnerships give youths the chance to work toward bettering their community. It's frustrating just to see problems and not be able to do anything about them. Partnerships get you out of the sidelines and into the game.

Youths and adults both have a lot to offer. Adults have experience and youths have a positive energy that generates fresh ideas. That's an effective combination that you wouldn't have with either group working alone. Both gain something from the other. Youths get the chance to make themselves heard in an adult world, and adults get a chance to be inspired by some youthful energy.

Adults offer their help in a partnership and youths offer their services in return. It's like a good relationship. Each one complements the other.

FROM: Loring Leifer
SUBJECT: Camp Letters

"Dear Mom and Dad:

"How come you haven't been sending lots of letters. I have sent you three. Something tells me my counselor Sherman is reading the mail. I know he reads the postcards. Mom, my counselor is so strict it is sickening. It is worse than living in a prison camp. Send permission for me to come home. I hate camp and my counselor. Love, Loring. P.S. Sherman, listen hear Fatso, you had better send this letter. (Mom, this is just in case he reads it.) P.S.S. Please send me up some hard fresh peaches and plums and other fresh fruit. We don't get any at camp."

I wrote this letter home from camp when I was in the fourth grade. When my parents recently showed me the letter, I was horrified at how little I had changed in the course of more than three decades. Camp was my first experience away from home, and I responded the same way I have to any new thing in my life since—with melodramatics, suspicion bordering on paranoia, and wild, empty threats. Then, when it looks like I have no choice but to adjust to the new situation, I order some small pleasure that might help me get through it after all—like a crisp, fresh peach or plum.

for adults only

Many people insist that they can't remember what it was like to be a youth, but this is only because we are afraid to admit how close we still are to being children. We have succumbed to *adultism,* a condition characterized by thinking that we operate on some higher plane than youths. Maybe we've slowed down or gotten more cautious, or transport more luggage—but we are essentially the same. Keep this in mind when starting youth/adult partnerships:

Youths are just new adults and adults are just old youths.

tips and tricks for managing youths
Don't expect more from the young people than you would from another adult. In much the same way that minorities feel they have to be better than their white counterparts to get the same rewards, young people do too. When a young person shows up 15 minutes late for a meeting, an adult will think, "Ah hah, a slacker. Irresponsible kid." When a fellow adult shows up 15 minutes late, the same person will think, "That's understandable. They've got deadlines and pressures and schedules." So do young people.

Make sure that you don't hold the young person to a stricter standard than the adults. Young people have many other commitments and pressures that cry for their attention. They often work long hours at schoolwork and jobs on schedules that would wipe out us more mature adults. And they will agonize more over their performance than an adult. In dealing with any new relationship, there is a caution or tentativeness. You both watch closely for signs that this might not work out. Don't exaggerate this tendency and expect the youth's performance to exceed that of adults.

Conversely, don't excuse all indiscretions just because you are dealing with a youth. Some of the survey respondents commented that they couldn't find fault with young people. When asked to recount the dumbest thing a youth has ever said to you, one respondent claims, "I realize I am much more gracious with young people than adults. I can't think of something I would classify as dumb from a youth, but I can think of several from adults." Sometimes adults tend not to expect enough from young people.

Treat youths as individuals, and don't make one youth represent all youths. Young people will put enough pressure on themselves. They understand that adults may carry negative images of young people and may generalize from the behavior of a few. Don't add to it by making them feel that they must speak for or represent all youths. You wouldn't do that to another adult. Assure the young people that you are interested in their individual opinions and don't expect them to embody an entire population. "When I was involved in my first partnership five years ago, we began proudly including ONE youth on our committee to be the voice of all youth," says Nancy Wayne, Ed.D., a psychologist at the Marblehead Counseling Center. "I fortunately caught myself early on and included others. Similarly, I have been the lone woman on a committee where I would not want to be seen as the voice of ALL women."

Be careful about interrupting. Youths get discouraged easily. Let them finish their ideas. For the partnership to work, young people must feel that they are valued and respected by adults. In many of their outside relationships, this respect is lacking and they are inherently wary of adults. When interrupted by an adult, they will tend to stop talking (sometimes permanently). To prevent this and create an environment that fosters equal participation, adults need to be hypersensitive about interrupting a young person and young people need to be encouraged to persevere with their point despite adult interruptions. Both parties need to respect others in their right to voice opinions without criticism or censure.

Remember that your role in a partnership is not to *parent*. While being a parent may be the most important role that any adult can play, the purpose of youth/adult partnerships is to give young people a different way to relate to adults. Parenthood implies nurturing and teaching. Partnership implies sharing information. Getting outside of relating to young people as children can be challenging—even for those adults who have never been parents. Nancy Wayne reminds herself when working in partnerships with young people, "I am not the caregiver, but a colleague; not the parent, but a peer—with my own adult identity. Because I so enjoy youths, as a professional and a parent, I've worked hard to establish the fine line between being one of the kids and the adult. So, it's difficult at first in a partnership to shift yet again, but it is well worth it."

Don't move too fast. Remember that this is all new for the young people. Don't move too fast without explaining the reasons for actions taken. Rushing through meetings can be a sign that adults are still trying to control the actions of the group.

watch your mouth
Sometimes adults use phrases and expressions, whether consciously or not, that annoy young people. Like an annoying drip of water, these expressions can erode a relationship and are red flags to young people that they are not being treated as partners.

thoughts from Loring

I don't have children, but I find myself relating to Michael as a mother. Michael does not wear coats. The temperature is 24 degrees; he's wearing a long-sleeved cotton shirt—and shivering. "I can't believe you're not wearing a coat," I say with the same incredulous tone a deli waiter would use as he looks at my plate and says, "You're not going to eat your pickle?"

"You're on a long list of people who say that to me," he says, disappointed. I've gone parental on him again. In the Promise Project, if Michael catches a cold, it's not my fault. I remember my first job at a newspaper where there were several older women who sang to me a regular refrain, "Wear a sweater or you'll catch your death of a cold." This used to annoy me, but at some level, I knew they were worried about me because they cared. I hope that Michael understands this, but I vow next time not to mention his coatlessness.

Be alert for words that intimidate or diminish the contribution of youths. Young people will be quick to detect biases and negative attitudes. Sometimes, adults aren't aware of how their language can diminish young people. Phrases like "You're so smart for 15" carry hidden messages like: you're not bad, considering you're an incompetent teenager. Imagine the same comment delivered to a colleague of a different race or gender. In many ways, learning to accept young people as true partners requires the same valuing of diverse contributions that would be required for adults of different backgrounds to work together.

thoughts from Michael

A dad of a friend of mine asked to go out with us one night. He said he'd go part his hair down the middle and mess it up. How strange the world would be if adults strutted around busting green hair and grunge wear. I think it would seem pretty stupid and the kids would turn around and wear the opposite. Style is just a cycle says the fashion editor.

Be careful about using words or phrases that young people might not understand. The language of the non-profit sector is riddled with terms that may bewilder a newcomer. Words like *advocate, consensus-building,* and *facilitate* aren't going to mean much to most young people. Neither will sentences laden with acronyms.

Think twice before using expressions like:

• When I was your age (I used to walk 10 miles to school, through dense woods, in the snow). Youths today have their own hardships, like metal detectors, gangs, drugs, AIDS. Don't try to impress them with how rough it was when you were a kid. You may lose in this game of one-upmanship.

• Oh, those stupid kids. If you wouldn't say it about the young people with whom you are working, don't use it to describe others.

• Sentences that contain a lot of words like Must, Should, and Ought.

• I demand respect.

• I suppose you think you're being funny? Rhetorical questions may be great in debates, but when dealing with others, they rarely accomplish anything other than annoying the listener.

A simple rule is think if you would speak to another adult like this, and if you wouldn't, don't say it to a young person.

pet peeves of youths Based on an informal survey of youths, here are some adult behaviors that most irk young people and cause them to feel disempowered:

• Putting on a superior or condescending attitude.

• Conveying that they know youths are irresponsible, rude, inconsiderate.

• Forgetting how they felt when they were young, and being insensitive to teenagers.

• Trying to psychoanalyze youths, like trying to figure out why youths drink.

• Ordering or assigning young people to do only small tasks.

• Being patronized, like getting praised just for showing up.

• Trying to play the role of a youth. When someone tries to act like they fit in, but it is playing a role and not natural. An adult saying, *What's up dude?* or *Grody to the max.* Adults who don't ordinarily dress in grunge attire suddenly showing up in super baggy pants, a tee-shirt with holes, and uncombed hair.

taking adults aside

Adults are sometimes insensitive to their own behavior with young people. Despite their best intentions, adults still tend to speak more often than young people, interrupt their sentences, frustrate their involvement, and cause them to withdraw from participation.

A normal part of training is to take adults aside before an intergenerational meeting with young people to form some guidelines. Here are some suggestions:

- Remind them that the goal is to create an atmosphere conducive to open discussion and to allow younger voices to color the organization.

- Ask the group to name some of the common courtesies or guidelines for such discussions and record the responses on paper for all to see.

- Review the list to make sure each item is understood and discuss the implications for the impending interaction.

- Following the intergenerational meeting, reconvene the adult group to describe what happened, analyze lessons learned, and assess how it might be improved.

Conversely, this approach works equally well with young people.

ten commandments for adults

John P. Kretzmann, the director of the Neighborhood Innovations Network at Northwestern University, has proposed 10 commandments for involving young people in community building. Here they are:

1. Always start with the gifts, talents, knowledge, and skills of young people—never with their needs and problems.

2. Always lift up the unique individual, never the category to which the young person belongs. It is "Frank, who sings so well" or "Maria, the great soccer player," never the "at-risk youth" or the "pregnant teen."

3. Share the conviction that: (A) Every community is filled with useful opportunities for young people to contribute to the community. (B) There is

thoughts from Loring

Michael never ceases to surprise me in our working together. For one, I've been surprised at how useful Michael is in suggesting alternatives to some of my own shortcomings. Michael and I both tend to procrastinate. One day, he told me about reading a book, Surfing the Himalayas, and how it helped him to act more quickly. We talked about how the impulse to do things perfectly kept us from action. We would put tasks aside waiting for just the right moment. He wouldn't clean up his room until every surface was piled with possessions and he had the time for a wholesale cleaning. After reading the book, he began to just put a few items away when the impulse struck.

The next week, I tried the same tactic. Instead of waiting for a time when I could return all my phone calls, I started calling people the moment I remembered. I sat down and wrote a postcard the day I got one from a friend. I let Michael influence my own behavior and felt more productive by the end of the week. Maybe I'll even have time to read Surfing the Himalayas.

I've also been surprised at how much two very different people can have in common. We both warm to people slowly—starting out quietly and warming to non-stop talking. We both like sushi and the Allman brothers, and don't like Hemingway or chocolate. We are both are the type who will let the other guy win in tennis.

I try to keep our similarities in mind when I start to go parental on him.

no community institution or association that can't find a useful role for young people.

4. Try to distinguish between real community building work and games or fakes—because young people know the difference.

5. Fight—in every way you can—age segregation. Work to overcome the isolation of young people.

6. Start to get away from the principle of aggregation of people by their emptiness. Don't put everyone who can't read together in the same room. It makes no sense.

7. Move as quickly as possible beyond youth advisory boards or councils, especially those boards with only one young person on them.

8. Cultivate many opportunities for young people to teach and to lead.

9. Reward and celebrate every creative effort, every contribution made by young people. Young people can help take the lead here.

10. In every way possible, amplify this message to young people: We need you! Our community cannot be strong and complete without you.

be open to surprise

"Be open to surprise" is the Promise Project's 11th commandment. If you stand back, you will invariably be surprised at what young people can accomplish. Cindy Ballard, executive director of the Coalition of Community Foundations for Youth, discovered this at a conference. "We challenged the community foundations to bring at least one young person to a conference. Forty young people attended. They planned activities around the metropolitan area, led panel discussions, manned registration tables, and worked as staff. It lightened our own load tremendously and improved the conference. They also thought of things that we did not—like setting up a message board and helping to locate people to deliver messages."

chapter nine

FROM: Michael McLarney
SUBJECT: Surviving the Fall

I wish you wouldn't worry about me getting hurt on a bike. I went biking yesterday and had a great time. I fell three times but didn't get hurt. That probably won't help your fear of me getting hurt, but I just wanted you to know that we do hit trees and fall into puddles. It animates the ride more and gives you a few laughs and aches.

Michael

FROM: Loring Leifer
SUBJECT: Surviving My Fear of Your Falling

In some warped way, I think you are trying to comfort me. I am touched by your reassurance, but still worried. I have a confession to make. When you suggested riding your bicycle to our meetings, I wondered how much experience you've had riding in traffic. Can you handle potholes, a squirrel running in front of your bike? I am a rather morbid person. Life seems tenuous, a constant assault of accidents waiting to happen. I want good things to happen to you, and I worry that I might be the cause of bad things.

I resist the impulse to suggest, "Why couldn't your mother just drive you over here?" I already relate to you too much as a parent. I feel guilty that the Promise Project is taking time away from your school work—or to just hang out with friends and be a kid. Easily, I can envision myself typing up your resume or helping you fill out college applications—even if you would never think to ask such a favor. I feel somehow responsible for you. I want to protect you from bad things—like falling off your bicycle. I suspect this is not conducive to partnerships.

an ode to failure

We have a tendency to want to protect those we care about from failure. But we forget that failure is the first step towards success. Thomas Edison spent years of his life searching for a filament for the light bulb that glowed. For years he tested 6,000 different types of filaments until he discovered tungsten. After discovering this metal that glowed a reporter asked him how it felt to have finally succeeded after 6,000 failures. Thomas Edison replied that there was no actual failure, rather he viewed his search as a 6,000-step process to success.

We live in a society that rewards success, but it is only by continuing to fail that most people ever reach success in the first place. Failure should be celebrated instead of being equated with inadequacy or rejection. Failing means that you are *trying*, that you are acquiring new information.

There are many different ways you can go about learning. The best is getting your hands dirty with actual contact. When learning how to ride a bike, anybody can tell you how to dodge a rock, but you'll take the lesson a lot more seriously after you hit that rock, flip off your bike, and sprain your wrist. After that you will definitely avoid those rocks. You learn how to ride by falling. You learn how to walk by tripping.

remember to let young people fail

If you see a young person crossing in front of a speeding train or acting in a way that will derail the organization, of course, you need to step in. *But make sure that you are stopping them for this reason and not just because you want to prevent them from making a mistake.* You should be protecting the project at hand, but if young people never fail, you may be controlling too much. You are preventing them from learning from their failures. We all learn more from failure than from success. Ask Edison.

In a youth/adult partnership, adults should let young people fail.

We've all heard a lot lately about the joys of risk taking. Literature in the business and non-profit sectors abounds with material on how willingness to take risks goes hand in hand with creative problem solving. So we are encouraged to be brave and face risks to suc-

thoughts from Michael

I had an appointment to meet Loring at one of the UMKC computer labs. I went to the building, and the door was locked. So I went home. When Loring called to ask me what happened, I told her the building was closed. Then she laughed and said she sure hoped not because she was calling from inside the building. I thought, oops, I should have tried another door. I learned that I shouldn't give up after just one try.

ceed. However, it is only by developing a healthy attitude toward failure that we will have the confidence to take risks in the first place.

the right response to wrongs Equally

important in the success of partnerships is how adults respond to failures.

After all, adults will fail, too. They don't always keep promises, act sensitively, or make wise choices. Adults need the same freedom to fail as young people do. If they recognize some of the benefits of failure and have a less negative attitude toward failing, then perhaps young people won't be so judgmental when adults stumble.

There is a wise, old saying: "Good judgment comes from experience; experience comes from bad judgment."

The way you respond to failures will determine whether failure becomes a learning process in the partnership or a permanent barricade to it. Let's say the young people in an organization plan a program and things don't turn out as expected. The attendance is low, and people don't take part in planned activities.

You could respond by saying, "That's too bad. We'll never do this again" or "Let's sit down and talk about what we have learned from this." The former response sends the message that this was an embarrassment that should be avoided again in the future. The latter message says this event is a learning experience from which something positive will arise.

Oscar Wilde used to insist, "Nowadays most people die of a sort of creeping common sense, and discover when it is too late that the only things one never regrets are one's mistakes." He understood the up side of making mistakes.

If you are to find your way out of a maze, you probably would have to run into a few dead ends first. Perseverance will pay off. Just keep on searching for the right way. If you stop making attempts at success, you may assure yourself that you will not run into any more dead ends, but you will not reach success.

Scientists deal day in and day out with failure, but they expect it. All scientists have dealt with a failed experiment. They don't always get the desired outcome, but use the failure as a lesson.

The Wright brothers didn't get their first airplane off the ground. They learned from what

thoughts from Loring

We had our moments in writing this book where we both contemplated trading the other one in for a new partner. Just ask Michael about the time I drove him to a committee meeting—over a curb and into some bushes. On more than a few occasions, I sent Michael to meetings without giving him the right address or scheduled a meeting in a place that was closed at the appointed time. Then there was the time I insulted one of his beloved mountain-climbing metaphors. The nearly unflappable Michael came close to shaking his head at me.

For me, there were times when I wondered with impatience when Michael was late in contributing work "why couldn't he just drop out of school and not go to college so he could spend more time on the Promise Project?" When we first divided up tasks, Michael planned to interview several organizations, then write accounts for the book. After seeing little action for several weeks, I, probably sounding a bit short, asked him what was the problem? He, with unwavering patience, explained that being in classes all day made it difficult to call adults during office hours. This hadn't dawned on me. (He was happy to take on more research and let me do more of the daytime phoning.) Then there was the time Michael spent three days trying to get a modem hooked up to his computer and patently refused my offers of help, even though I was the one who insisted he get the modem to make communications between us easier. (I solved that one by insisting I just wanted to look at his computer, which he graciously allowed.)

We both learned from and laughed over our mistakes and our missteps. Michael became the designated driver and checker of office hours. I got to be the chief caller and computer wizard.

67

went wrong and tried again. They used failure to inspire them instead of defeat them. In their failures, they found a blueprint for trying again.

Jonas Salk in developing the polio vaccine spent 98 percent of his time documenting the things that didn't work until he found the thing that did work.

These people saw failure not as a sign of defeat, but as a prelude to success, a stage or step to be understood and then used to best advantage. They embraced failure and manipulated it as a creative agent to drive their work.

Youth/adult partnerships are a new arrangement. They could be regarded as an experiment in social science. And like most experiments, they may not work the first time. When failures occur, they should be treated as the stepping stone to success.

Perhaps if we kept in mind that many extraordinary people expect failure, adults wouldn't try so hard to protect young people from failure. Young people especially need to be encouraged to try things that may not work. After all, the proper management of failure breeds success. That means looking at your failure optimistically and saying, "Hey, I sure learned a lot from that one."

To create this positive response to failure, all levels of the organization have to support this premise. This can be especially hard for paid staff who work under the credo that it is their job to make the adult volunteers succeed. They need to be reassured that their jobs aren't riding on the uniform success of young people.

When entering a partnership it's not all going to be warm fuzzy compliments and smooth-running operations. After all, we're not machines. We are human, and we will make errors. The best thing we can do is learn from these errors.

There will be days you may wonder what possessed you to try this social experiment. Adults will wonder why young people can't act more like adults. And young people will roll their eyes and regard their elders with the utter disgust only found among youths.

Youths are not as experienced as adults. Youths cannot be expected to work as efficiently as adults. They will make mistakes. Through these mistakes, each partner will learn how to work more effectively and forgivingly

You need to bump into dead ends to keep moving. Just keep on bumping until you find a way.

FROM: Michael McLarney
SUBJECT: Tinkering with the Evaluator 2000

Loring, yesterday I was looking at our chapter on evaluating a partnership again. I sat and thought meditatively, as I often do, and pondered how do you evaluate a partnership? I thought of scales, but that didn't work. I thought of different tests, but there aren't any tests compatible with all partnerships. Wow, how tough could this be? I snapped my fingers and nodded my head. I had a vision. A large cloud-like bubble formed above my head. I saw the tool for evaluating partnerships. It gleamed like a brand new Ford. It had an internal combustion, 58-horsepower engine that fueled the machine. All you had to do to get the Partnership Evaluator 2000 to work was switch on the choke, pull the cord, and rev the throttle. To get an evaluation you fed in a partnership description that answered a few questions. Did you get along? Did you successfully divide the labor and, if so, did you both accomplish what you set out to? How well did youths and adults communicate? What were the partnership's benefits? After you feed this information into the propeller in the bottom, the engine spurts and rumbles. Finally, it shoots out a number from the side. The number will be from one to ten, one being "needs improvement" and ten "outstanding." I popped the bubble above my head and got to work on the machine immediately. Today I went to True Value to pick up some supplies. The Evaluator 2000 is coming along great except it needs more oil and only runs on premium unleaded fuel.

FROM: Loring Leifer
SUBJECT: Typoe Champion Gloates Over Victory

Sometimes, I suspect that you are more dad-like than kid-like. I get the feeling that you are worried about my welfare and feel responsible for my enjoyment of this project. When we were doing the final spell check on a draft of the manuscript, I only suggested a Typo Contest to see who made the most errors so you would have something to do while I went through the manuscript. As you made hatch marks on the scorecard under my name, I could see you troubled with the fact that I was the Typo Queen, having made so many more than you. You kept trying to get out of the contest, saying, "We don't have to play this game any more. I can stop at any time." You seemed much more embarrassed than I to have my shortcomings exposed. I have the feeling you would rather be the one with the 70 typos instead of the 19. Then, when we went to turn in the manuscript, you insisted on driving me home, saying, "I'm not comfortable with your walking alone at night." You perpetually remind me that all of us are part youth/part adult within ourselves.

is it working?

the second most important question to ask yourself after "why bother with a youth/adult partnership" is "how can we evaluate whether that partnership is working?"

Ask yourself: Can you laugh together? Can you disagree without raising your blood pressure? Is your hair grayer? Have you learned a new language? Do you find yourself smiling for no apparent reason? Has your pace quickened? Is membership rising?

Every organization that enters into youth/adult partnerships should have in place some mechanism for measuring the success of the partnership as well as the organization's endeavors. It should involve carefully defined objectives; how work toward these objectives will be measured; and an assessment of the final outcome. What changes in behavior or attitude occurred?

The Resource Development Institute outlines some key concepts in an evaluation program:

- Identify the general objectives of the program and prioritize them.

- Identify specific goals to be achieved to reach each objective and indicate how you will know when each goal has been achieved.

- Prepare a timeline indicating important steps along the way and when each goal and objective will be reached.

- Prepare an organizational chart and assign responsibilities to particular individuals for achieving goals.

There are lots of questions to be asked, so design a process for testing and re-testing your efforts. By stopping to evaluate, you'll get the opportunity to tune and refine your programs. Not-for-profits as a whole are beginning to recognize the importance of building a quantifiable case for their efforts. It's a lot easier to get funds if you can demonstrate your successes. This goes for youth/adult partnerships as well.

signals of success

Here are some areas where you can get an indication of whether your efforts are on target:

- **Enthusiasm.** Look for what gets people excited (shown by lots of ideas generated, paying attention) and look for what gets them down (sighs, side looks, side conversations).

- **Curiosity.** Are young people asking a lot of questions? That's a good sign. It means they are engaged. If you ask for questions and there aren't any, it probably means that interest is low. Be alert for blank looks, long silences.

- **Clarity.** Do people understand their responsibilities and assignments? Do they agree on common goals? If you asked adult and youth members to each describe a project, how close would the descriptions be?

- **Growth in membership.** If the group grows, it means something is going right and that young people are communicating their enthusiasm to their peers. If it doesn't grow, that's something to check out. It may not be tuned into the needs of those it's serving.

- **Lots of laughter.** In lieu of high salaries and personal advancement, enjoying yourself can go a long way to maintaining commitment to a cause.

Sometimes the signs of success are more subtle. Sometimes, success is measured by shifts in attitude. Success can be when you begin to look at your organization not as a group of adults and youths trying to work together, but as a *team* composed of *equally important partners,* each making an essential contribution.

"research is what i'm doing when i don't know what i'm doing."

– Wernher von Braun

icebergs in paradise

Young people won't always tell you that they are not happy with the way the partnership is working, so you have to be alert to the signals they might send you. While your children could win a Nobel Prize if they ever start a category for argument and contradiction, they will often have a difficult time communicating their displeasure to adults.

"I feel uncomfortable confronting adults," "I just avoid them when I'm unhappy with adults," say several survey respondents.

So, don't expect young people to express dissatisfaction directly. Be sensitive to more subtle clues. Signs of trouble include:

- **Drop in attendance.** This signals that the program isn't meaningful to them or they don't feel a sense of ownership.

- **A previously animated youth who becomes quiet or shy.**

- **Not looking you in the eye.**

- **Rowdy or challenging behavior.**

- **Complaining about work to be done.** Even if the complaints are unfair, look for the dissatisfaction or frustration that may be behind them. Pay attention to those "but" statements. "Yes I'm happy, *but* ..."

- **Not performing agreed-upon tasks.** This could mean that the youth just has too much to do, but if the youth had been performing similar tasks in the past and suddenly stops, it's a sign that the youth feels the task is demeaning or unreasonable or confusing.

- **No follow through.** What percentage of projects gets carried out versus falling by the wayside? What is the reaction to projects that don't get done? We can't accomplish everything we set out to do, but a lack of concern about this indicates trouble. A lot of volunteer groups don't have good follow through. If it's poor, check out the commitment to the project, morale, leadership of the group. Look at whether the task is too ambitious and/or too big.

shared lessons
All organizations need to have a process in place to communicate their complaints and concerns in a non-threatening way. This might mean asking members to write down their grievances—either signed or unsigned—and setting aside some time in each meeting to address them. By bringing them out in the open, the group gets to see how prevalent or serious are its problems. There's an old saying, if one person calls you a jackass, ignore it. If two people call you a jackass, think carefully about their accusations. And, if three people call you one, buy a saddle. If only one of many youths complains that the adults are patronizing, then perhaps the situation is isolated. If two complain, it is time to explore further...

By building in a means to air grievances, you increase the opportunity to learn from your mistakes.

We can save ourselves a lot of hassles by learning from other people's mistakes and progress. Say you're strutting down the street and you pass a local pedestrian. The local is just hanging back relaxing by the newspaper stand and sipping his coffee. As you walk by with your new sneakers gleaming white on new terrain you hear the local. He tries to stop you. "Hey, excuse me I got something to tell you." You glance up at him and see his baggy pants and dirty hat and conclude that it would be better to ignore this guy. Anyway what could this guy know that would possibly be of importance to you? Splash! you fall into a small manhole and ruin your new jeans and sneakers. The local peeks over at you floating in the sewage and says, "HAD something to tell you. But now I guess you'll just have to learn on your own." Bobbing up and down in the muck, you wished you had listened to that strange-looking guy.

Most people have valuable knowledge that they could share. After all, that's the very foundation of youth/adult partnerships. Young people need more opportunities to share their valuable knowledge with adults. We hope that this book will encourage you to create those opportunities and grow your own partnerships. At least, maybe this book will help you avoid falling into a muddy hole or help you laugh and learn together when you do. And, as we leave you, we also hope that you will find your own youth/adult partnerships as rewarding as we found this one.

epilogue

FROM: Loring Leifer
SUBJECT: Mashed Potatoes

Michael, I only hope that others who go on to work in partnership relationships will learn as much from their partners as I have from you. I do know that I have found our experiment to be highly entertaining and enlightening, and, in a mysterious sort of way, I am learning more about myself.

In my rush to get the job done, I sometimes forget to use my imagination. You are always there to remind me with your amusing metaphors and novel comparisons. Last week, I wondered if you thought we were closer to the finish line than I did. You said you saw the book as a mound of mashed potatoes on a plate at the school cafeteria. The potatoes were ready to eat, you said, but the server was shaping and molding them on the plate so they would hold the gravy just right. I am still laughing at the image of both of us trying to make sense of this mass of mashed potatoes. In your gentle and indirect way, you reminded me that I am sometimes too reluctant to let go of the potatoes. In my own writing in the future, I will try to do more describing through comparisons. I'm sure that my own writing will improve through our working together.

You have also inspired me with your exercises to overcome your own procrastination. The next time I start to place a piece of paper in my in-box, I'll remind myself that the job could be completed with less time and trouble than it would take to refind the document later. I'll just conjure up that image of you before we printed out the manuscript. After deciding that I had dawdled too long over the formatting, you pointed a water pistol at me and in your most commanding voice, warned, "Hit Control Print or I'll Shoot." Anyway, I wanted to thank you for making sure that we got the job done. If left alone, I would probably still be here debating the merits of Avant Garde versus Futura.

You were always the first one to try to see an issue from another person's perspective. I hope that some of your patience and sweetness has rubbed off on me as well. I know that from now on I will be ready to be surprised by teenagers. I'll ask more questions and come to fewer conclusions. And will be grateful to you for that luxury. This partnership writing has certainly been one of my most enjoyable (and educational) endeavors. We may not get rich from it in money, but rich in experience.

Your partner, Loring

epilogue

FROM: Michael McLarney
SUBJECT: Are We Really Finished?

Loring, I guess the finality of the project is kicking in, but I don't want it to be over. The book has been such an enjoyment to work on. This whole week I've been thinking about it and about how this project just leads to others. I've made contacts at a national magazine, been invited to speak at a symposium, and gotten an award for the project at a school assembly. When I first looked into the project, I really saw it in a one-dimensional view. I saw a writing job as a writing job, but now I see it three dimensionally. This project has opened up doors that I never knew existed.

After six months of working, I've learned a few things from you. Besides learning how to save a file on an IBM computer and how to spend thirty minutes on formatting, I've learned some things that are more valuable. I've learned to trust adults more. I used to revere adults from afar. They seemed a distant reflection of what I would become. Now I've learned differently. I've developed a respect and comfort with adults. I've learned to move from my position playing with the dust beside the computer to stealing your seat and writing an introduction to a chapter. I still revere you as an accomplished writer who has more experience than myself. But now I revere you from your own seat. I've moved into the project with a new confidence that allows me to take charge.

You've shared your wisdom with me on some of the most obscure topics of bike riding to the most relevant of writing. I think that the project has really helped me develop as a person and a writer. I've admired your style of writing, minus the typos, and even tried to mimic it, including the typos.

My experience with you has increased my level of comfort with adults. I owe a lot to you because you've given me a lot of respect. We both developed a common respect that allowed us to understand each other better. So finally in conclusion I've seen the image of an old woman commanding me to write and assigning demeaning jobs change to a friendly partner who is happy to lend her keyboard to my hands.

Your partner, Michael

resources

Promise Project
301 East Armour, Suite 605
Kansas City, MO 64111
Phone: 816.753.3398
Fax: 816.753.6019
Web site: www.kcconsensus.com
Contact: Jennifer Wilding
The Promise Project promotes partnerships between young people and adults. It offers training programs and consulting services to organizations seeking to start or refine youth/adult partnerships. Its training programs include the Partnership Retreat, "Partnerships 101" training, and the Youth as Trustees and Youth in Governance curricula that was developed by the Community Partnerships with Youth, as well as this book.

Activism 2000 Project
P.O. Box E
Kensington, MD 20895
Phone: 800.KID.POWER
Email: ACTIVISM@aol.com
Contact: Wendy Schaetzel Lesko
Activism 2000 Project is a resource center created to encourage young people to achieve lasting solutions to problems about which they care deeply. Its publications include *No Kidding Around! America's Young Activists Are Changing Our World & You Can Too,* as well as publications about youth initiatives on issues like AIDS, deforestation, violence, and homelessness.

Coalition of Community Foundations for Youth
1055 Broadway, Suite 130
Kansas City, MO 64105
Phone: 816.842.4246
Contact: Cindy Ballard
The mission of the Coalition of Community Foundations for Youth is to strengthen the leadership capacity of community foundations to improve the lives of children, youth and families.

Community Partnerships With Youth, Inc.
2000 North Wells Street
Fort Wayne, IN 46808
Phone: 219.422.6493
Contact: Anne Hoover
CPY promotes active citizenship through youth and adult community partnerships. Its training curricula are called "Youth as Trustees" and "Youth in Governance."

Constitutional Rights Foundation
601 South Kingsley Drive
Los Angeles, CA 90005
Phone: 213.487.5590
Email: crfcitizen@aol.com
Contact: Civic Participation Department
The mission of CRF is to be activists for the rights of young people. One of its publications is *The Role of Youth in the Governance of Youth Service Programs.*

National Child Rights Alliance
P.O. Box 61125
Durham, NC 27705
Phone: 919.479.7130
Contact: Jim Senter

New York State Youth Council
55 Grant Avenue
Albany, NY 12206
Phone: 518.459.6648
The New York State Youth Council offers training materials, including *How to Start Your Own Youth Council,* a 30-page booklet that describes how to set up the council, draft bylaws, secure funding, and recruit members.

Resource Center for Youth and their Allies (RCYA)
25 Boylston Street
Jamaica Plain, MA 02130
Phone: 617.522.5560
Contact: Jenny Sazama
Booklets available are: "Building Relationships," "Get the Word Out!" "Leading a Youth Worker Resource Group," "Listening to Young People," "Tips & Guidelines for Allies to Young People."

Resource Development Institute
601 Walnut
Kansas City, MO 64106
Phone: 816.221.5000
The organization provides evaluation consulting services, helping organizations to improve programs and build resources.

Washington Youth Voice Project ESD
112 2500 N.E. 65th Ave.
Vancouver, WA 98661-6812
Phone: 360.750.7500 ext. 362
Youth Voice works to strengthen youth involvement in schools and communities by helping students and adults to gain the needed skills and resources to work together effectively and efficiently. It offers tip sheets on action planning, training, burnout, recruiting youth volunteers, creating partnerships, addressing stereotypes, listening to language, defining roles, apathy, and liability issues.

William Lofquist
Development Publications
P.O. Box 36748
Tucson, AZ 85740
Phone: 520.575.7047
A youth development consultant, Lofquist is the author of *Discovering the Meaning of Prevention* and *The Technology of Development Workbook.*

Youth As Resources
1700 K Street, NW, Second Floor
Washington, DC 20006-3817
Phone: 202.466.6272, ext. 151
Contact: Maria Nagorski
YAR connects youth to their communities to improve community life nationally and internationally through the spread of youth-led service initiatives. It offers training and materials to help start Youth as Resources programs. The *Youth As Resources Training Manual* gives step-by-step instructions on how to implement YAR and includes a video and instructions on how to recruit a board, build a funding base, etc.

Youth on Board
YouthBuild USA
58 Day Street, Third Floor
P.O. Box 440322
Somerville, MA 02144
Phone: 617.623.9900
Contact: Karen Young
Youth on Board is a project of YouthBuild USA that encourages young people's voice and ensures that this voice is heard and heeded in all programs and organizations that involve young people. It offers the SpringBoard Training Institute for Young People and BoardBlazers, a technical assistance program for boards that involve young people. A publication on "Youth Governance: 14 Points to Involving Young People Successfully on Boards of Directors" is also available.

bibliography

Brukardt, Mary Jane, *Are You Ready? A Resource Guide for Enhancing Youth Participation,* draft edition, Wisconsin Partnership for Youth (Racine, WI: The Johnson Foundation, 1995).

Community Action Plan: Today's Youth—Tomorrow's Future Johnson County Task Force on Drug & Alcohol Abuse, Inc., and Johnson/Wyandotte County Teen Advisory Council.

Kretzmann, John, and McKnight, John, *Building Communities from the Inside Out: A Path Toward Finding and Mobilizing Community Assets* (Evanston, IL: Center for Urban Affairs and Policy Research, 1993).

Lofquist, William, *The Technology of Prevention Workbook: A Leadership Development Program* (Tucson, AZ: Associates for Youth Development, 1989).

Peer Prevention Partnership Project: Training of Trainers manual.

Schai, Ruthanne Kurth, "The Roles of Youth in Society: A Reconceptualization, *The Educational Forum* (Winter 1988).

Styles, Melanie, and Kristine Morrow, "Understanding How Youth and Elders Form Relationships" *Public Private Ventures* (6/92).

The Role of Youth in the Governance of Youth Service Programs, Constitutional Rights Foundation.

Whiting, B. B., & Whiting, J. W. M., *Children of Six Cultures* (Cambridge: Harvard University Press, 1975).

Young People Creating Community Change and *Adults as Allies,* Kellogg Foundation.

Youth in Governance: A Board/Committee Member Curriculum, Community Partnerships with Youth, Inc. (Fort Wayne, IN: CPY, 1994).

acknowledgments

the Promise Project would like two thank two important groups of people: members of the committee that oversaw the development of *Younger Voices, Stronger Choices* and the individuals who read the first draft and provided valuable advice.

The Promise Project Book Committee worked for more than a year to identify the need for a book like this, agree on the contents, hire Loring and Michael, and oversee production. Their wisdom and hard work made this book possible. The group consists of:

The two co-chair: **Karen Bartz,** Hallmark Corporate Foundation, and **Janice Benjamin,** Career Management Center. Members are **Cindy Sesler-Ballard,** Coalition of Community Foundations for Youth; **Ryan Hardy,** Lee's Summit High School; **Julie Metzler,** Young Audiences, Inc.; **Paulette Riley,** YWCA of Greater Kansas City; and **Valerie Snitz,** Shawnee Mission East High School.

The book readers who generously provided both advice and encouragement are: **Janet C. Baker,** Janet Baker & Associates Consultants, Kansas City, Missouri, a company that helps organizations identify and serve key stakeholders.

Sue Bloemer, upper school principal at Pembroke Hill School in Kansas City, Missouri.

Myra Christopher, Midwest Bioethics Center in Kansas City, Missouri, which promotes ethical decision-making in health care by consumers, professionals, and organizations.

Phil Jachowicz, regional service director of the Boys & Girls Clubs of America in Chicago, Illinois, which helps youths become responsible citizens and leaders.

Robert Long, program director at the W.K. Kellogg Foundation in Battle Creek, Michigan, which helps people help themselves through the practical application of knowledge and resources.

Monica Meeks, executive director of STOP Violence Coalition in Kansas City, Missouri, which is dedicated to the prevention of interpersonal and family violence.

Leon Moon, project director of the 4-H After School Activity Program in Kansas City, Missouri, which is a partnership to provide educational enrichment programs to youth and families in public housing.

Jared Shirck, a student at Lee's Summit High School in Lee's Summit, Missouri, and member of the Promise Project Governing Board.

Janet Wakefield, director of Community Partnerships with Youth, Inc., in Fort Wayne,

Indiana, which promotes active citizenship through youth and adult community partnership.

Nancy Wayne, Ed.D., a psychologist at the Marblehead Counseling Center in Marblehead, Massachusetts, which provides education and counseling, and serves as a catalyst for addressing issues facing individuals and families.

The authors would like to add their own special thanks to the Promise Project Book Committee for choosing us to work on what has become a most endearing assignment and to **Jennifer Wilding,** program manager of the Promise Project, who made our jobs easier by providing us information and resources along the way and, more importantly, cheering us through the throes of composition and making us laugh when we despaired.

success form

Let us know what your program has learned from youth/adult partnerships. We will share this information with future readers. Just fill out the form and return to:

Promise Project c/o Kansas City Consensus, 301 E. Armour, Suite 605, Kansas City, MO 64111
Phone: 816.753.3398 Fax: 816.753.6019

Name:_____ Organization:_____

Address:_____ Phone:_____ Fax:_____

City/State/Zip_____

What does your organization do?

_____
_____
_____

What did you learn from your partnership effort?

_____
_____
_____
_____

How has the organization changed?

_____
_____
_____
_____

What can you tell us that might help others?

_____
_____
_____
_____
_____
_____

Would you like to be included on the Promise Project mailing list?

Yes ___   No ___

notes

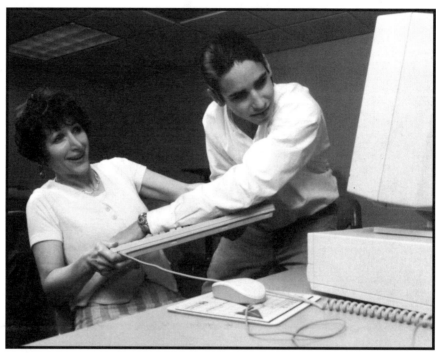

Issues of control often surface in youth/adult partnerships. Here, Loring and Michael "discuss" who should have access to the master file.